HOW TO BE
A PERFECT
CHRISTIAN

THE BABYLON BEE

HOW TO BE A *Perfect* CHRISTIAN

YOUR COMPREHENSIVE GUIDE TO FLAWLESS SPIRITUAL LIVING

MULTNOMAH

How to Be a Perfect Christian

All Scripture quotations, unless otherwise indicated, are taken from the Holy Bible, New International Version®, NIV®. Copyright © 1973, 1978, 1984 by Biblica Inc.® Used by permission. All rights reserved worldwide. Scripture quotations marked (esv) are taken from the Holy Bible, English Standard Version, ESV® Text Edition® (2016), copyright © 2001 by Crossway Bibles, a publishing ministry of Good News Publishers. All rights reserved.

Hardcover ISBN 978-0-7352-9152-2
eBook ISBN 978-0-7352-9153-9

Cover design by Kristopher K. Orr; cover image by ClassicStock, Masterfile

Published in the United States by Multnomah, an imprint of the Crown Publishing Group, a division of Penguin Random House LLC, New York.

Multnomah® and its mountain colophon are registered trademarks of Penguin Random House LLC.

Library of Congress Cataloging-in-Publication Data
Names: Babylon Bee, LLC.
Title: How to be a perfect Christian : your comprehensive guide to flawless spiritual living / the Babylon Bee, LLC.
Description: First edition. | New York : Multnomah, an imprint of the Crown Publishing Group, a division of Penguin Random House LLC, [2018]
Identifiers: LCCN 2017045191| ISBN 9780735291522 (hardcover) | ISBN 9780735291539 (electronic)
Subjects: LCSH: Satire—Religious aspects—Christianity. | Christian life. | Christianity and culture. | Christian life—Humor. | Christianity and culture—Humor.
Classification: LCC BR115.S26 H69 2018 | DDC 277.3/0830207—dc23
LC record available at https://lccn.loc.gov/2017045191

Printed in the United States of America
2018—First Edition

10 9 8 7 6 5 4 3 2 1

Special Sales
Most Multnomah books are available at special quantity discounts when purchased in bulk by corporations, organizations, and special-interest groups. Custom imprinting or excerpting can also be done to fit special needs. For information, please e-mail specialmarketscms@penguinrandomhouse.com or call 1-800-603-7051.

Soli Deo gloria

CONTENTS

Introduction

SO YOU WANT TO BE A PERFECT CHRISTIAN

f you're reading this, we want to congratulate you. In the vast sea of Christian books written by talented authors to strengthen your faith, supplement your walk with Christ, and teach you valuable truths about God and Christian living, you picked this one. Really—great job.

Maybe this book caught your eye because you just know, deep down, that you have what it takes to be a perfect Christian. Or perhaps you already feel that you're amazingly special, sinless, and beautiful, no matter what the Bible has to say about that. Or maybe you went on an impulsive Christian book–buying spree while browsing the Internet late one night and have no recollection of ordering this guide or the collected works of Karl Barth that showed up on your doorstep like magic this morning.

Whatever brought our paths to cross, we at *The Babylon Bee* want to welcome you on a glorious adventure to become a perfect Christian—**which you will assuredly be by the time you finish reading this book.** The storms of life may howl and the rocks of doubt may threaten to dash you to pieces, but if you cling to the one sure hope that the potential to be perfect lies within you, you will succeed.

What is a perfect Christian? We asked three biblical scholars and theologians this question,* and in our extensive research, we found that **a perfect Christian is one who conforms to the man-made standards of the Christian faith in any given age.** Conforming to the status quo is the goal. Living out your faith in the way cultural Christianity dictates is the only way you'll truly be satisfied in your Christian walk.

So if you want to be perfect, as the great theologian Steven Curtis Chapman once said, "Saddle up your horses, we've got a trail to blaze." Let's go!

You may not know the road to Zion yet, but that's why we're here. We'll point out the way along the tried-and-true path to complete Christian perfection. We'll walk alongside you as you take each painstaking step toward igniting the divine spark within until you arrive at the peak of the Christian life, delighting in the knowledge that you are amazing. We'll be here holding your hand, like that creepy kid at junior high

---

* There is a chance they were all cult members in a remote compound in Idaho, but they seemed like pretty nice guys, so we are confident they are correct.

group who would do it "as a joke" but then never actually let go through all fourteen choruses of "Lord, I Lift Your Name on High."

We want you to be such a great Christian that bards will write songs of your greatness for years to come. A few decades from now John Piper will use your life as an example of radical, Christ-centered, God-saturated, all-satisfying sacrifice in one of his books. Maybe a supercool worship band will even write a song about you, using a deep, esoteric metaphor about a hurricane or a blazing inferno.

See, to become perfect, you need to be baptized in the glorious waters of Christian culture. Cultural Christianity is an amazing thing. It's a perfectly preserved bubble of everything that made the church awesome in 1950, like gospel quartets, three-piece suits, and pipe organs, with all the good vibes and positive energy from the sixties. Those who are submerged under its depths never surface, but instead they are transformed day by day into the radiant image of the modern American Jesus.

"Hold the phone!" you might be exclaiming aloud to the book you're holding. You're probably wondering what's wrong with the Christian life that you're living right now. Well, if you're like many Christians, you struggle with sin. You aren't ever sure that you're good enough. You know God is a God of grace, and yet you don't always measure up. You don't always feel like a good Christian, let alone a perfect one.

If reading this has made you realize your Christian walk is less than a victorious one, don't worry. You're not alone. Many Christians just trudge through life without ever attaining to the higher levels of the Christian faith. The root of your problem is that **you're not trying hard enough to become perfect by your own efforts**. You're trying to do the Christian life by the grace of God, allowing Him to gradually change you by the power of His Word. This works for some people, but it's not befitting a true believer.

No, the true believer desires one thing above all else: **conformity to the status quo of the modern church.**

Luckily for you, we're here to make that a reality in your life. We're going to get you plugged into a church that's tripping over itself to make you amazing. We're going to help you worship like a truly spiritual person, hands held up in victory and swaying like a palm tree in a hurricane. We're going to help you clean up your life from anything the modern church has infallibly declared to be a sin, like listening to secular music or doing yoga. Finally, we'll help you share your newfound perfection with others through evangelism and political outreach.

And then, when all is said and done, you'll be able to stand on top of the summit of living the perfect Christian life and lift your hands triumphantly, like the silhouettes on those stock images your church uses during the worship time.

Ugh, we're literally tearing up right now thinking about how amazing you're going to be when we're through with you.

You'll be the poster child for Christian perfection.

Let's not get ahead of ourselves though. You'll certainly stumble. You'll certainly fall. You'll certainly lose your step and make fools of us all. But even through your imperfections, we'll be here to pick you up and speak words of affirmation into your life throughout your walk with the Lord.

Remember, as Jesus said, it is the journey to Christian perfection that counts, not the destination.

JOINING THE RIGHT CHURCH

If you've ever felt a modicum of displeasure at your church, even if just for a fleeting second, get out of there immediately and find a new one.

—C. S. Lewis

You want to be a perfect Christian, and that is a noble goal indeed. But first things first. It's impossible to get to the maximum level of holiness if you're currently attending a church that is focused on the wrong things, namely, on anything other than *you*.

Paul David Tripp once wrote that church is a place "where flawed people place their faith in Christ, gather to know and love him better, and learn to love others as he designed." It's a nice sentiment, but it's also completely *wrong*. Flawed people? Excuse us, Paul, but we're trying to become absolutely perfect here, not hang out with a bunch of messed-up folks. We don't need that kind of negativity in our lives.

And neither do *you*—which is why you're reading this book.

We know you may have feelings of loyalty or attachment to the humble, local expression of the body of Christ that you've been a part of for years. You need to rid yourself of these unholy emotions. It's time to step back and objectively evaluate whether or not your church is properly equipped to encourage you on your sacred quest to become the ultimate manifestation of impeccable spirituality.

So open your eyes and start looking for the red flags that indicate your church isn't a spiritually fulfilling congregation.

Some of the most common warning signs that your church isn't conducive to your personal growth into a perfect Christian include **a pastor who preaches sermons that make you feel uncomfortable, a worship experience that centers your attention more on God than on your own feelings, and a church staff who refuse to incorporate the advice from the thousands of helpful comment cards you've left over the years.** These kinds of churches are dangerous. If you find yourself treading water in a similar spiritual wasteland, it's time for your very first step toward spiritual awesomeness: church shopping.

Your journey to living a flawless Christian life begins today! Ditch that group of hopeless losers who have been holding you back and instead find a church that's built around *you*—and all of your needs and desires.

According to recent research, every single town in America has a minimum of 6,521,587 churches to choose from, so you've got your work cut out for you. You actually have a better chance of winning the lottery while getting struck by lightning than of picking a good church near you on the first shot. So it's a great thing you have this book to help you out.*

In the olden days of the apostles (circa 1950), there were just a few churches in town. If you wanted to visit one, you had to put on your Sunday best and build up the courage to march right in the front door without having a clue as to what to expect. **What a nightmare.** But—thanks be to God—these are the days of the World Wide Web, a magical portal to all kinds of great resources (and almost nothing bad or degrading—lots of wholesome stuff, mostly). So you get what the church fathers could only dream of: the benefit of shopping around online for a church from the comfort of your own home.

Approximately twenty years after the magical Internet sprang up out of nowhere and revolutionized modern communication and commerce, churches discovered they, too, could create a website and spread the good news through the magic of technology. So the first step in selecting a new, improved local body of Christ is to Google churches nearby and start separating the wheat from the chaff.

Try search terms like "church near me that has cool coffee

---

* We again commend you on your impeccable discernment in choosing this piece of literature. Some suckers are reading a Tim Keller book right now with all his C. S. Lewis quotes and Lord of the Rings excerpts. Chumps, all of them. Keller books are a dime a dozen, while this book is going to go down in the annals of history as a turning point for Christianity. Think *Pilgrim's Progress* or *The Purpose Driven Life*, then kick it up a few levels, and that's the book you're holding right now. Not quite canonical, but the next best thing.

bar" or "church near me that isn't weird or stuffy" or "good trendy church near me that uses T-shirt cannons." Just have fun with it. You ought to use any search terms you think will help you sift through the millions of nonpersonalized churches in your area and find a true diamond in the rough: a church that emphasizes and cultivates the historical Christian virtues of convenience and comfort.

Your search will likely return approximately four billion hits, but don't worry—we'll sort through them together.

The first thing to look at is the church's name, which provides all kinds of clues to help rule out churches that stubbornly refuse to cater to your felt needs 24/7. A lame name is a big no-no.

What you're really looking for is a church with a name that sounds like either a **retirement community** or a **natural disaster.**

Whispering Pines Community Church or Cedar Grove Church, for instance, are probably churches that are worthy of your presence. These names could easily be confused with an apartment complex, a mini-mall, or a delightful retirement community—consider this a sign that you're on the right track.

Alternatively, the church should have a name reminiscent of a destructive act of God. For example, consider checking out churches with names like Granite Deluge of Life, Floodwaters Collective, Whirlwind Love Fellowship, or Blazing Inferno Church. If the church sounds like its name alone could crush you under the destructive weight of its awesomeness, you're probably going to be in for an exciting, you-centric experience.

What you should be very cautious of is any church with a name that brazenly indicates an affiliation with any of the major evangelical denominations, just hanging out there for the whole world to see. First Baptist Church, Grace Methodist Church, or New Life Presbyterian Church are examples of churches to avoid. After all, you're looking for an *organic, custom-fit experience,* not a stuffy old denomination. If the church meets you halfway with a name like Hurricane of Life Baptist, proceed, but with caution.

Speaking of Baptists, this would be a good time to get into some specifics about **denominations.** There are several denominations to choose from. So let's break down what each of them has in store for you.

If you do decide to go with a **Baptist** church, it's certainly a noble heritage. Baptist churches have been around since, well, John the Baptist. It's right in his name. This means that Baptist churches have literally been around since before the New Testament, so you know you're going to please God by attending one of His elect church denominations.

Be warned, however, that Baptist churches come with a lot of rules, even though you do get really great potlucks chock-full of superhealthy food. First of all, you can't consume any drink stronger than a Diet Mountain Dew within fifty feet of a Baptist church. Trust us, it's in the church's bylaws.

Also, the closest you're allowed to get to dancing is an awkward swaying motion during a really powerful praise chorus or hymn, and even that's a real gray area, so be really, really careful.

If the Baptists sound too stuffy, you could try the **Pentecostals,** who allow you to get drunk, but only on the Holy Spirit (it's not as awesome as it sounds). Pentecostalism was conceived by a group of Christians who were totally high after attending a particularly groovy ABBA concert in Southern California in the fall of '79. As a result, this denomination is totally cool with dancing, especially during worship songs, sermons, announcements, the offertory—it's pretty much *Soul Train* at all times when you're among a charismatic congregation. Just be sure to pack your own tambourine or dancing ribbon so you'll fit right in when wild, noisy gyrations begin erupting all around you.

For those of you who consider yourselves truly righteous, you might want to choose a **Presbyterian** or **Reformed** church.* These guys don't have time to mess around, so you'd better fall in line once you join their ranks. So much as a single hand raised in the air during an awesome, obscure hymn you've probably never heard of can land you a disciplinary hearing

---

* Of course, never, ever say you chose a Reformed church. Always say that God, in His sovereignty, predestined you from eternity past to attend said church, for His glory alone.

with the deacons—and you do not want to mess with them. There are stories of Reformed deacon boards "disappearing" problem parishioners and erasing any evidence of their existence from all public records. They're cool with beer though, as long as it's a craft microbrew with a high enough alcohol content to put down a mature African elephant.*

Mainline denominations can be a nice choice because they won't really hold you to any theological standards. Mainline doctrinal statements consist solely of questions. But by the time you've finished reading this sentence, odds are that every mainline church near you will have closed its doors due to bleeding beliefs and declining attendance. So that's probably not a solid option for you anyway.

If in your searching you happen to unearth a disquieting website featuring Times New Roman font, late twentieth-century design principles, several spinning GIFs of Satan's likeness, and links to hundreds of articles about how the NIV was created by an alliance between Beelzebub and the Illuminati in an Area 51 research lab, you've stumbled upon a King James–only church. Feel free to check them out, but make sure you bring your ESV, NLT, or *The Message* translation with you when you go. They are really reasonable and level-headed when it comes to discussing translations other than the Authorized

---

* We'll have more to say about beer later in the book.

Version from 1611, and dialoguing with these folks can be a joyful and edifying experience.*

So you could try any of the above denominations, but then you'd end up being a total weirdo and not a cool, spiritual, holy, *perfect* Christian.

Wait . . . what?

Yes, we tricked you. Did you think it would be that easy to become a perfect Christian?

If you've been paying even the slightest bit of attention, you ought to understand that you should avoid all of the crazy name-brand quacks and just jump right into a **nondenominational** paradise.

So go back to your Google search. Click on the most promising nondenom link you see with a sweet name, and let's check out their online presence.

In addition to a killer church name and a lack of denominational identity, a church that will help you achieve perfection will have a **superslick website**. Any local body that hasn't updated its upcoming-events page since the fall picnic of 2002 should be rejected out of hand. Their lack of Web 3.0 skills obviously indicates they don't care about Jesus at all. You want up-to-the-minute information telling everyone what the pastor is up to, live streaming video for those Sundays when you just

---

* Please note: *The Babylon Bee* bears no responsibility for your well-being should you attempt this maneuver.

don't feel like going to church, and tons of upcoming events and programs for your entertainment.

Once you manage to find a website belonging to a run-of-the-mill nondenominational church displaying acceptable web design prowess, there are a few other key indicators to look for to make sure it's the kind of place you want to be on a Sunday morning.

One of the marks of a healthy church website is the frequent use of heavily filtered stock images that perfectly encapsulate that aesthetic you need to truly worship the Lord. If the church site you're checking out has pictures of people with a realistic level of attractiveness, close your Internet tab right away and try again. Ideally, the church you target will feature several images of young, unrealistically attractive models smiling and raising their hands as if worshipping with reckless abandon or desperately trying to flag down a passing car.

Another important mark of a healthy church is that it **does not have a statement of faith**. If there is a list of dogmatic beliefs anywhere on the website, no matter how well it's hidden, run. Flee. Stay very far away. At most, allow for the church to have a vague page titled "Our Journey" or "The God Story" that lays out a very fluid set of general teachings in poetic cadence. A beliefs page that simply lists some U2 lyrics is all right by us too, as long as they're not from that awful *Pop* album.

Unacceptable Statement of Faith Excerpt	Acceptable Statement of Faith Excerpt
We believe the Bible to be the Word of God, perfect in all its parts, truth without any mixture of error, and useful for all areas of the believer's life.	In the locust wind comes a rattle and hum Jacob wrestled the angel And the angel was overcome

Remember, you're going to be stuck at this place for months or, in rare instances, *years*. You want a place that's not going to pin you down too rigidly on any of your key doctrinal beliefs. Their positions should be vague enough that you can slip by with your shifting, undefined understanding of the Christian faith completely intact. We know it's difficult to pass on a church that checks all the right boxes but fails in this regard, but we're looking out for you, and you have to trust us. *The last thing you want is to be forced to take a stance on a core doctrine of the Christian faith.* This is for your own good, brother or sister in Christ!

Navigating through the website's various pages and menus, you ought to find their logo prominently displayed (ideally, it should take up the entire top half of your screen, but we won't be too rigid on this). Make sure the church has a logo that is just straight *fire*. Literally. It should have fire in it. Or water.

Glorious, blazing fire or cool, refreshing water. But barring these two metaphorical images, something really modern and ornate is ideal. A simple cross or clip-art image of a Bible is so ten years ago and not befitting a cutting-edge body of Christ or a Christian as awesome as you.

Finally, surf your way to the part of the website where you can check out the vast array of ministries and services your potential new church has to offer. If you find only Sunday morning services, Wednesday night Bible studies, and a small group or two listed, that's just not gonna cut it. This is a huge red flag, and you've got to cut this one loose. A respectable church should offer more upcoming shindigs than any local club, venue, or arena. We're talking no less than three dozen wild events in the next month. That's a bare minimum.

Their ministries should be wide and varied, with ultra-specific groups tailor-made for every age level, walk of life, race, color, creed, nationality, hobby, gender, hair color, and species under the sun. After all, can we really call a local gathering a New Testament church if they don't offer a middle-aged male former Ping-Pong enthusiasts ministry?

Now, with any luck, you've narrowed down your search using the magic of the Internet. You've found a church that looks as though it could help you along the path to perfection. Great!

The next big step is to perform a drive-by. You want to scope the place out in person before committing to anything or meeting anybody who might want to talk to you.

Hop into the family minivan and cruise on by your potential new Sunday gathering place. At this point, if the commute takes any more than three minutes, abort the mission. Church commutes of five, ten, fifteen, or more minutes are simply not convenient, and we've already established that convenience is what it's all about. In addition, if the church is more than three minutes away from you, why hasn't the pastor launched a satellite campus right down the road from you? Why don't they just put a big pop-up on their site saying, "We don't value you"? Any church with less than twelve satellite campuses is probably dying anyway.

Pull up to your prospective church, situated a short distance from your home, hopefully with plenty of parking and a gorgeous, well-manicured, expensive-looking property. Ideally, the main church building will be of modern construction, no older than five or six years. The more indistinguishable the structure is from a shopping mall, nightclub, or theme park the better.*

Look out for noncontemporary warning signs like steeples, crosses, hymnbooks, or any other old-looking funny business that might indicate anything traditional or time tested. Stained-glass windows or evidence indicating the pastor is preaching methodically through a book of the Bible should also raise your suspicions.

This is a great place to tell you all about **church signs**. You

---

* An Ohio man once shopped at a shopping mall for over twenty years before realizing it was actually a church. That church's seeker-sensitivity game was seriously on point!

know, the marquee out in front of many churches, facing the street. The church sign is an ancient art dating back to the days of Solomon's temple (see 1 Kings 6) and is really a canvas on which pastors and other important church staff bring to life some of the modern world's very best artistic expressions in the form of puns that are equal parts witty and inviting.

A church sign might say something really clever like "Brush up on your morals to prevent truth decay!" or "1 cross plus 3 nails = 4 given." The puns should be funny, but this is no laughing matter—there are countless stories of people being converted on the spot by anointed church-sign puns. So feel free to pass your holy, righteous judgment on any church based solely on the quality of the wordplay on the marquee. Remember: a puntastic church is a quality church.

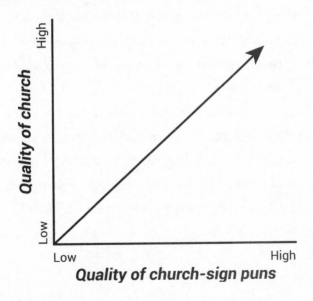

In any case, this might be a moot point, because the kind of church that suits you is probably too hip and avant-garde even for a sweet sign out front.

And there's only one type of church that can be awesome while lacking a church sign.

We are talking about the holy grail of modern churches, friend: **the megachurch.**

The only sign a megachurch should have is a cutting-edge modern art piece proudly declaring its name in big stainless-steel, sans-serif letters. Ideally, the church also has wacky inflatable air dancers elegantly announcing to the surrounding neighborhood: "Hey! We exist! Please come here. Please!" Balloon arches, giant rotating arrow signs, bounce houses for children *and* adults, and big inflatable gorillas are all acceptable forms of outdoor advertising as well. And they're also key indicators that the church you're looking at has big bucks to spend, meaning they're probably doing pretty well—always a definite sign of God's blessing.*

After all, you're looking for a church that can encourage you toward excellence. How are they supposed to do that if they don't have an annual operating budget larger than most third-world countries? How are they going to help you become a perfect Christian if they don't run the church like a Fortune

---

* Source: TBN.

500 business? On what planet could a church ever effectively declare Christ to your neighborhood without having tens of thousands of people show up for worship each week at their main campus and dozens of franchises?

If the church has a lit name, a slick website, no statement of faith, a modern building, and membership of at least fifteen thousand each week, then great! You may have found the place where God will have your material needs met and keep you entertained (at least until a cooler, more modern church comes along). But for now, slip out of your crusty old church without so much as a goodbye, and get ready to visit your new home at whichever of the nine weekend service times is most convenient for you.

We want to take a moment at this point to let you know you're doing a great job of becoming a perfect Christian. **You're well on your way.** Lots of people would have started to question whether or not choosing a church is really all about finding a place where you're comfortable and catered to. But not you— you're sticking this out because you know God wants to give you His best blessings now!

You really are special. Just sit there for a moment and think about how amazing you are. We'll wait.

Done? Great. Then let's gear up to walk you through your first Sunday morning visit inside your potential new church!

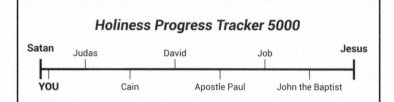

Holiness Progress Tracker 5000

Using patented motion-tracking technology developed in conjunction with LifeWay Research, The Babylon Bee's proprietary Holiness Progress Tracker 5000 will provide you with helpful updates as you move along on your personal path of sanctification over the course of this book.

Looks like you're somewhere between Satan and Judas at this point. Not good!

Best get to reading chapter 2 if you care about your eternal fate at all!

Two

WORSHIPPING LIKE A PRO

Now throw yo hands in the ay-err, and wave 'em like you just don't cay-err.

—The Apostle Paul

You've scoped out the church's website. You've performed recon on the building. You might even have prayed over your decision, declaring a hedge of protection around your choice.

Now, it's go time. Select the service time that's most convenient for you, pile the family in your minivan, shine up your Christian fish decal, and get going. Don't worry, we're going along with you!

We begin with the drive to church. The goal for any church commute is to be late enough to miss most of the peppy opening worship song but not so late as to miss the funny video clip just before the sermon. So be sure to time your departure appropriately. Depending on how far away from the church you live, aiming to arrive during the five-to fifteen-minute window after the service starts is a pretty good rule of thumb.

As you pull into the parking lot, a smiling man in an orange vest will direct you to the nearest available parking spot.* Be supernice to this guy and tip him well. He is your ticket to a primo parking spot on Sunday morning.

As an interesting historical note, the orange parking lot ministry vest is a traditional sign of authority in many Christian denominations. These vestments grant the wearer special powers, such as knowing when to point you to the special visitor parking section and when you're a regular who needs to have some humility by parking 3.2 miles away in the overflow parking at the Burger King across town (don't worry, most orthodox churches have trams to shuttle you up to the door, as the apostle Paul commanded). So make sure to "respect the vest."

It's very important that all fights taking place inside the family car cease before you enter the parking lot. You're at church now, for heaven's sake. It's imperative to act like Christians whenever you're in the field of vision of other church-goers. Any conflicts can resume the moment you leave the parking lot after the service. Your aim is to look as holy as

---

* If the church does not have parking lot attendants, leave. Reread chapter 1 and try again.

possible as your smiling family approaches the building. Make sure your children, in particular, understand how important this is! If you've got to bribe them with new video games, candy, trips to Disneyland, so be it. It doesn't matter what state their hearts are in as long as they appear to be little smiling cherubs as soon as you crack open those foyer doors.

Walking toward the front doors of the church, there should be a group of people milling about. This is the welcome team. This crack squad of perpetually happy people will be ready and waiting to cheerily wish you a good morning and ask how your week is going. Your instinct will tell you to avoid eye contact or try to time your approach so as to slip by when they are busy welcoming other families, but either is futile. The welcome team *will* engage you, come hell or high water. They are well trained for this.

Important note: When they ask how you are doing, always say "fine." Did your dog die? The answer is "fine." Are you having doubts about your faith? "Fine." Are you terminally ill? "Fine!" Never, ever let on that anything is wrong or you might have to start connecting with people on an authentic level. This would be a disaster.

One of the primary rules of being a perfect Christian is to always give off the appearance of perfection even when things are falling apart on the inside.

Appropriate Responses
to the Welcome Team

How You're Actually Doing	Appropriate Response to Welcome Team Asking How You're Doing
Fine.	**"Fine."**
You had a really bad week at work.	**"Fine."**
You're pretty sure you got salmonella from an undercooked chicken casserole at yesterday's church picnic.	**"Fine."**
Your house went into foreclosure and you're going to have to move into a 3' x 3' crate on the side of the interstate by Tuesday.	**"Fine."**

The welcome team, for their part, is a special bunch of people. They're one rung up the spiritual gifts ladder from the parking lot ministry folks. Their skill set is primarily comprised of looking uncannily happy, saying "God bless you!" to thousands of people every Sunday, and shaking more hands than most people will ever shake in their lives.

We're not saying their job isn't important, but they're definitely not the apostle Paul or St. Augustine in terms of significance. Never get sucked into joining this ministry, as they don't get nearly the number of accolades the pastor or worship team does.

You're staring down the welcome team, and now, here it comes: the primary litmus test of the morning that will forever decide whether or not you should make this church the place where you will achieve perfection. We're talking about **the quality of the church swag they give away to visitors such as yourself.**

Church swag varies wildly in quality. Ten years ago, churches could get away with just giving visitors a warm handshake, a doughnut, and a cup of coffee. We've got two words for that kind of giveaway in today's highly competitive church era: *bush league.*

What you're looking for is high-end gear here: aluminum water bottles, American Apparel T-shirts, expensive vacation giveaways, and NFL tickets. Freebies like these let prospective visitors know the church is serious about helping them attain true godliness and they're not just messing around. In the book of Revelation, Jesus even threatened to remove the lampstand of the church at Ephesus due to their lack of high-quality handouts for visitors. The Lord definitely means business when it comes to baiting the visitor hook with awesome swag.

In addition to lavishing expensive gifts on you to gain your loyalty, the welcome team will give you a church bulletin. The bulletin is its own literary art form, on par with the significance of an ancient Greek epic poem and the great American novel. Researchers have discovered that every church bulletin in existence contains no less than three hundred spelling or grammar errors. If you find one with less than that, hang on to it—it's gonna be worth some money someday.

Once the welcome team stops badgering you and you're weighed down with a half-dozen bags overflowing with awesome freebies, great job! You've made it past the first line of defense. You should now be in the church lobby. You might look a little out of place, reading this book while you're standing in an unfamiliar church foyer, but rest assured that we're going to get you through this ordeal in one piece.

Look around. You should see several prominent features, standard to all churches built over the past thirty years. The first of these is the **coffee shop**.

The church coffee shop is essential to the life of the Christian church. Before churches began installing coffee shops in the early 1990s, absolutely no fellowship or serious discipleship took place at church. People marched into the building, were yelled at by a preacher, sang "Just as I Am" for thirty minutes while doing this weird up-and-down motion with their hand, and marched straight home without uttering a word to one another. Thankfully, someone got the bright idea that, without a place to sit in trendy-looking chairs and sip caffeinated beverages, the church foyer would continue to be a barren and empty land of fellowshipless silence after church. Thus the church coffee shop was born.

The church café is like an inferior version of Starbucks, which is already an inferior version of real coffee shops. So it's pretty low on the coffee shop totem pole, like most Christianized versions of other things—a fact we all know, but all perfect Christians know to never admit this. Church cafés have sanctified names like Higher Grounds, Holy Beans, or HeBrews and feature mediocre drinks with similarly redeemed titles. Pick up some hot chocolates for the kids if you want to, since it usually supports a good cause like an upcoming short-term mission trip or funding the pastor's new Porsche, and then hightail it out of there.

Passing by the coffee shop, you should come to the church **bookstore**, a retail wonderland filled with all the most popular Christian books at full MSRP as well as the pastor's latest book, prominently displayed near the front of the establishment. The security room will be watching you closely as you pass the bookstore, so be sure to pick up a copy of the pastor's book for each member of your family, and keep them at the ready as the pastor will probably preach from it during the sermon, instructing you to turn to certain pages and read aloud with him as he delivers his message.

Now, also make sure the church bookstore has all of today's most popular Christian bestsellers, like adult coloring books, fifty-eight different versions of *The Purpose Driven Life,* and all 470 Joel Osteen books in print. This is how you know the church is serious about teaching the right kind of doctrine, and as a soon-to-be perfect Christian, you're gonna need all the doctrinal integrity you can get.

You've gotten your free swag, you've picked up your Lazarus Latte at the coffee bar, and you've perused the bookshop. **Now you're ready to enter the service**. Take a deep breath and head on in through the double doors in the middle of the foyer. Don't worry—we're in there with you!

Ideally, the auditorium (also called a sanctuary, worship center, or multipurpose room) will feature **heavy, billowing fog** seeping out of every door and window. In the sixth chapter of Isaiah, the prophet has a vision of God, and he describes the great throne room of the Most High as being filled with smoke. Hello, people! Can you say "fog machine"? Modern churches are simply trying to faithfully emulate Isaiah's vision as much as possible.

The stage should also feature **high-powered laser lights** blasting in every direction. It should look like an amusement park for cats or a Def Leppard concert. In addition to being rad visual stimuli, they also function as runway lights so the Holy Spirit knows where to land.

It is absolutely imperative there be **no outside light** allowed to intrude into the worship service. In the Bible, light is often used as a metaphor for sin, while darkness is often used as a metaphor for goodness and holiness, so it makes sense that the worship service be as dark as humanly possible. If your church has open windows that allow sunlight in, it may not be right for you (and we hope you haven't forgotten rule number one: *it's all about you*).

Although you'll be stumbling around in darkness at this point, you should be able to feel your way toward your seat. Hopefully, the place of worship you're visiting features a series of interlocking chairs, designed for maximum comfort, with multiple levels of adjustability. If the church has pews, the establishment is probably too old-school to effectively meet your needs as a Christian in the fast lane to righteousness.

If by some infinitesimally small chance you've fallen asleep while reading this book, wake yourself up and pay attention, because this is crucial: *where you sit in the sanctuary is one of the most important decisions you will make today or maybe ever.* Make one wrong move here, and your spiritual growth could be irreparably damaged.

The ideal spot to sit is about **three-quarters of the way back, next to an aisle.** This way, if the overpowered lasers set the building on fire, you'll be able to get yourself out of there while the poor fools sitting in the middle of the row burn to death. Plus, you can slip out of the service to use the restroom at convenient times, like when the offertory begins and the ushers start to take up the offering.

Under absolutely no circumstance should you sit in the front row. That row is exclusively for visiting celebrities or for the pastor to sit while he waits for the worship band to finish, that is, if the church doesn't have a greenroom in which he can wait, avoiding the worship time altogether. Sometimes the pastor's wife is allowed up there too, especially at those churches that list the pastor and his wife together on all their advertising, like the Reverends Ted and Grace Etherton.

Finally, make sure you're not sitting behind a lady with a giant hat. Every church has a handful of them. And if you plunk down behind one, you're going to have a poor view of the performances onstage.

You're doing great, Christian. You're seated at least three-quarters of the way back in the sanctuary, and you're lounging in the ideal spot in terms of temperature and comfort. With any luck, you're looking really spiritual to those around you (you've got the pastor's book out in plain sight, right?). You're doing church just the way God intended!

Now let us guide you through the **worship segment** of the modern church service.

As you walked in, you probably heard an upbeat song being played by the worship band. This is the opening tune, and no one really pays attention to it, since most of the church doesn't show up until halfway through the service anyway. If your church isn't up with the times, the worship band probably plays "Open the Eyes of My Heart" or "Come, Now Is the Time to Worship" here, but any church worth its salt is playing a song that came out last week to show they're modern, hip, and trendy. Either way though, this up-tempo number is there simply to get your feet tapping and let everyone know that church isn't stuffy and boring anymore. It's fun and hip!

Take a good, hard gander at the stage now, and let's get familiar with the **worship team**. You want to make sure before proceeding any further that your prospective church has no less than nine pieces in the worship band: drums, guitar, backup guitar, rhythm guitar, bass guitar, lead guitar, male vocals, female vocals, and keyboard. Go ahead, look for them and count them off. Each of these is crucial, and worshipping the Lord in Spirit and in truth can't occur if even one of these is missing.

Even if everything else up to this moment is totally on point with your new church, should all nine essentials not be present onstage, it's time to pretend you're getting an emergency phone call and book it out of there.

All three guitarists will sound as though they are copying absolutely every riff they play from a U2 song. This is known by clinical psychiatrists as The Edge Syndrome, an altered state of mind in which worship guitarists actually believe they are members of U2. Thousands of guitarists are affected each year.*

---

* If you believe you or a worship guitarist you know may be affected by The Edge Syndrome, please consult a medical professional immediately.

Every musician in the worship band also has a ridiculous amount of gear. We're talking a collection of three or four dozen expensive guitars, a massive amplifier, $40,000 microphones, and even guitar pedalboards the length of an NBA court.* Despite all this expensive equipment, you may notice that the bassist will only be plucking the lowest string of his guitar, playing the root notes of the song.† Bass riffs are for the Red Hot Chili Peppers and *Seinfeld* segues, totally inappropriate in a church setting, unless your pastor's as funny as Jerry Seinfeld.

It's important that every member of the worship band is unbelievably attractive, so your attention remains on them throughout the Sunday morning concert. They can't have any eyes wandering anywhere else, like at a hymnal or a Bible. The spotlight is on the worship band for a reason, so make sure to pay attention to them!

Also, make sure the singers are nailing incredibly complex harmonies in addition to ad-libbing nonsensical vocal fills throughout your worship experience. Is the backup female singer speaking in tongues or is she just improvising absolute gibberish? That's between her and Jesus. What you need to be concerned with is how spiritual the worship band is making you feel right now.

---

* No one is really sure why the guitarists need all this stuff, because they're usually a little shaky on playing a B minor barre chord. But they can definitely nail the opening riff of "Stairway to Heaven."

† A church bassist at a Delaware megachurch once ventured onto the higher D and G strings, and a church council burned him at the stake for heresy, which is why bassists are so careful about staying in line.

It's also important to understand that no member of the worship band reads music. Most churches have outlawed actual musical notation for fear that the little dashes and circles might be some kind of dark magic that would unleash a terrible demonic force on all of us or summon Cthulhu from his watery slumber. So it's a good thing really, for our own protection.

Any worship band worth its salt recognizes that **the worship leader is the most important person onstage.** He should have flowing hair that appears to have easily taken three hours to shape, an expensive brand-name T-shirt, a tasteful piercing or two, a few exposed tattoos, and maybe even an edgy hat, if you're lucky. He'll be leading the whole ensemble, nailing all four chords in perfect succession while singing passionately and prancing around with wild, dramatic body movements—sometimes without even looking at the words. He's got 'em memorized! How spiritual is that?

It goes without saying that the worship leader wears designer jeans. Did you think just anyone could go before the Father on Sunday morning in lame khaki pants or a nice three-piece suit? No, the Most High God demands our very best, and that means $450 jeans. Make sure to check out those trousers, and feel free to approach him after the service to ask how much they cost.

Take a minute and make sure the worship leader is firing on all cylinders.

Worship Leader Checklist

☐ Impossibly nice hair or sweet hat

☐ Risqué neckline

☐ Piercing(s)

☐ At least one visible tattoo (inner forearm preferred)

☐ Passionate, exaggerated undulations

☐ Designer jeans

☐ Rock-star presence

☐ Should attract all the attention

As the worship band wraps up its first song, the worship leader will inevitably smile at the crowd and ask you all to turn to your neighbor and recite some rich theological phrase like "Smile, God thinks you're amazing!" or "Neighbor, I got the victory!"

Friend, this is a test! Only baby Christians fall for this trap. Do not turn to your neighbor. Do not move. **Stand strong and stare straight ahead,** ignoring anyone who dares to approach you during this manufactured time of fellowship and greeting in order to shake your hand. Be a rock.

People will notice and will respect you for this. You're already making a name for yourself!

This church greeting time will mercifully end after no less than five hours of forced smiles and reluctant handshakes, and the worship band will slickly segue into their next song. Pay close attention to the smoothness of the worship band's transitions throughout their performance—studies have found a correlation between a worship band's ability to smoothly transition between songs and a strong gospel-centered church body. If the worship leader fumbles while trying to switch his guitar tabs over to the next page one too many times, you're probably in some kind of heretical organization or blasphemous cult.

Worship bands always, always slow the music down as the set progresses, so you're going to be faced with a midtempo number next, followed by a slow song or two. While the slow song was your cue to ask a girl to dance in junior high, in the modern church service it's your cue to **show everyone else how spiritual you are with wild displays of emotion and hand raising.**

This is important. If the congregation doesn't raise their hands during the powerful slow song before the sermon, they probably don't love Jesus. You can easily measure the devoutness of a church by how many people raise their hands, sway violently to the music, and start rolling around in the aisles. This is how the Spirit was manifested throughout the book of Acts, and He doesn't move any differently today. The more seizure-like convulsions, the more spiritual the church body.

So unless you want to look like a weirdo, get those hands up in the air. Don't just throw them up on the first blistering guitar riff leading into the first verse though—make the worship band work for it. On the powerful choruses, lift your hands high with abandon. On the subtler verses, tone it down a touch. When the bridge drops, you get a chance to really show how holy you are. Go for it with both hands and a feigned expression of emotion on your face. Sway side to side like a tree in the wind. If you open one eye at this point, you'll probably notice the people around you staring at you in awe that they're in the presence of one so holy.

As they should be.

Meanwhile, this Bon Jovi–inspired power ballad will start to wind down, and the worship leader will lead a breathy prayer while he quietly picks his guitar. Look down, eyes closed, and utter "Yes, Jesus," a few times in a hushed tone.

When he's finished (at long last), the lights will slowly morph from pitch black to a moody blue, orange, or purple.* Let us be the first to congratulate you—you've endured your first modern worship set and now you're ready for the meat and potatoes of this whole shindig: **the sermon.**

Once upon a time, blistering, fiery sermons were preached from great, ornate pulpits. But in the modern enlightenment era, preachers don't so much preach as they sit on a hip stool and chat with you for fifteen to twenty minutes. They want you to feel as though you and they are just kickin' it, chillin' at Starbucks or the aforementioned church coffee shop. Alternatively, they'll preach from a snazzy Plexiglas pulpit, showing

---

* If they don't have a whole spectrum of colored mood lights, they don't love Jesus.

how transparent and authentic they are. Either of these preaching implements is acceptable.

Now's a great time to size up **the pastor**. If he's any good at ministry at all, he's been hiding in the greenroom throughout the service, so this may be your first glimpse of the man himself. What's he look like? What kind of vibe is he giving off?

A good pastor is, first and foremost, a **great dresser**. He should look like a fashion model straight off the cover of a catalog. He'll be sporting a supertrendy outfit, much like the worship leader, but his wardrobe will be slightly more dignified and refined, so everyone knows he's the boss. The main thing is that he looks 100 percent on point, signifying that he is **the most important person in the room**.

The pastor gets bonus street cred if he sports a tattoo, preferably in Hebrew or Greek, so you know he's legit and has a past. Usually, the inscription is a single word, like *shalom, doulos,* or *agape,* probably because it's the only word the pastor remembers from seminary. The tat should be subtly placed on an upper arm, where it just kind of teases you with its presence every time he makes a gesture with his hands. Bask in his holiness and maybe some will rub off on you!

Now, the sermon itself begins in earnest. Usually, pastors kick things off with a few jokes or some witty anecdotes to break the ice. Sometimes, if you're really lucky, the pastor will perform a major stunt, like shooting himself out of a cannon, riding in on a motorcycle, or parachuting onto the stage through a retractable roof. Pastors since the time of Christ have been trained to really start working the crowd in order to hold everyone's attention for the next fifteen or twenty minutes. In fact, modern Bible scholars believe the apostle Peter's sermon on the Day of Pentecost kicked off with the man himself launching over the crowd on a dirt bike. Google it if you don't believe us.

In no circumstance should you easily offer laughter or applause. Make the pastor work for it. That's what he's getting paid the big bucks to do, and he really needs to be on top of his game if he is to garner your reluctant snicker or refined golf clap. You should be going for an attitude of aloof smugness as though you've heard it all before.

Good pastors use hand movements to make their points. **We want to see arms waving as if he's trying to get airborne.** If he doesn't look like he's trying to sell you OxiClean on a late-night infomercial, he's not trying hard enough. Pastors who simply stand near the pulpit and never wildly swing their arms around probably never went to seminary and might even be heretics for all you know. You have to be discerning!

The sermon itself ought to be organized in an easy-to-digest outline, preferably using **a helpful acronym.** If his sermon is focused on God's love, for instance, the sermon points should collectively spell out L-O-V-E. Expert pastors can even twist, stretch, and distort their sermon points to fit into a ridiculously long word like T-R-A-N-S-U-B-S-T-A-N-T-I-A-T-I-O-N. This is Basic Sermon Preparation 101, and it tells the audience he's done his homework and knows what he's talking about.

The other biblical way to write a sermon fit for a Christian such as yourself is to use heavy alliteration. The pastor ought to make all his sermon points start with an *S,* for instance, even if he really has to reach to make that last word start with the appropriate letter. It's been scientifically proven the Spirit won't move through sermons that are built on basic outlines of the text without any clever gimmicks.

As for the content of the sermon itself, **it's crucial to ensure your church regularly preaches through popular movies and hit TV shows.** Should the pastor ask you to turn to a particular verse in your Bible at the outset of the sermon, that's a major red flag. A good pastor knows there's a lot more spiritual truth in *Breaking Bad* than in the Bible.

Now, for some things you should **never** hear from the pulpit. Here is a helpful list of five blacklisted words you should listen for. If any of these pop up at any point during the pastor's sermon, pull a fire alarm, start flopping around on the ground like you're having a seizure, whatever—make any excuse to get out of there.

1. **Sin.** Sin is a no-fly zone as far as we're concerned. Watch out for clever euphemisms for the idea of sin too, like "oopsy-daisies" or "brokenness." Anything that implies you're not amazing just the way you are is simply un-Christian.

2. **Hell**. We're not opposed to the idea of the after-
life. For instance, we're great with the concept of
heaven. But hell is just a super-icky idea, and it has
no place being brought up in a Christian church
service. Let's try to keep things PG, people!

3. **Cross**. The problem with talking about the cross in
church is that it implies you're not wonderful just as
you are (see "sin" above). If the worship band has a
couple of mentions of the cross in their songs, you
can let those slide for the sake of poetry or metaphor or whatever—those lyrics are probably being
phased out of those songs, anyway. But actually
preaching about the cross is certainly going too far.

4. **Wrath**. There is only one verse in the Bible that talks
about God's character, and it says "God is love." Any
other characteristics like His wrath or holiness are
simply not scriptural ideas, and pastors who talk
about these things are really not being very nice.
We don't know why some continue to do it.

5. **Repentance**. What kind of goofy pastor talks about
repentance nowadays? Can you say "outdated"?
Any call to change your life is offensive to how
beautiful you already are and is in no way helpful
in your quest to become a perfect Christian.

As long as the pastor is careful to avoid no-go subjects like
sin and hell and also manages to remain entertaining through-

out his speech, you may be looking at an awesome candidate for a local church body to support your efforts to amaze God with your perfection.

There's still one more potential danger: **the altar call.** The altar call is a time-honored tradition in which the pastor begs people to please, please make some kind of decision for Christ. Usually, he'll have people raise their hand if they feel so led or come to the front before they're whisked away into a back room and loaded up with all kinds of free visitor swag.

The pastor will not end the altar call until he has met his salvation quota, so there's a good chance you'll be stuck there for hours while the Methodists get all the good seats at Chili's. It might make sense at this point to jump on the proverbial grenade for everyone and just pretend to accept Christ (even though you obviously already have) and raise your hand. You get free stuff, you look spiritual in front of everyone, the church's all-important numbers get beefed up, and everyone gets to leave church early. It's a win-win-win all around!

Before leaving the service, have every member of your family fill out a comment card, which you'll find on the seat back in front of you, and list every way the church failed to live up to the virtues outlined in this chapter. Feel free to go even further than we have—inform the church that the carpet is the wrong shade of purple or the worship set didn't include your favorite version of "Good, Good Father" that you learned at summer camp. Trust us: churches will really appreciate your thoughtful input, and you will come off as the superspiritual champion that you are.

Now, you've laid the groundwork for your newfound life of holiness by joining a church that's all about you. The worship experience leaves you with an addictive emotional high, the pastor whispers sweet nothings about how wonderful you are for fifteen minutes or so—you're going to get a weekly recharge every time you walk through those modern glass doors.

But as the old hymn goes, "Your hope is built on nothing less than your own amazing superawesome righteousness." Joining the right church and learning to look spiritual in front of other people are just the first steps.

Now the real work begins.

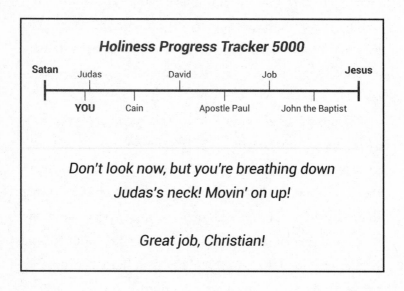

Holiness Progress Tracker 5000

Satan   Judas   David   Job   **Jesus**

YOU   Cain   Apostle Paul   John the Baptist

Don't look now, but you're breathing down Judas's neck! Movin' on up!

Great job, Christian!

Three

DOING LIFE TOGETHER

What you do in your private time is nobody's business but your own. But for goodness' sake, clean yourself up and act like a Christian when in the presence of other believers.

—J. C. Ryle

You've gotten through your first modern worship service, and if everything has gone well, you now have a whole waitstaff of church personnel at your beck and call, ready to help you out on your journey to somehow become even more awesome than you already are.

Wow!

We don't want to jump to any premature conclusions, but we can say with some confidence that you're gonna be such a perfect Christian. We just have a really good feeling about it. And with a full team of pastors and leaders who just want to love on you and affirm your lifestyle choices, no matter how unbiblical they may appear on the surface, you've got all the support you need to reach out and claim perfection.

Unfortunately, there's a major obstacle that prevents many believers from discovering their limitless potential. The sad fact of the matter is that **your Christian life isn't lived alone**. It's lived in community with other Christians, who inevitably don't follow Jesus as well as you do.

Sucks, right? Totally. We know you probably want to run away to your safe space, well out of reach of your fellow disciples of Christ. We understand. Those chumps can only bring you down. But unfortunately there's really no way around it.

Take heart. With some guidance from us, your life lived in the community of your fellow believers can be redeemed. In fact, if you're really committed to perfection, you can exploit their fellowship into a vehicle for your continued advancement toward holiness.

Let's pull back the curtain and let you in on a little secret: one of the tricks to being a perfect modern Christian is to make sure you **never let anyone get close enough to your life to see what a mess it is below the surface.** The key to true Christian authenticity is to **look** authentic without actually making yourself vulnerable. Share stories of being late to things because your children insisted on praying for their grandparents or other precocious but nonthreatening explorations of God's love, and be sure to call your family life "beautifully messy." But keep any actual mess, shortcomings, or failures well hidden.

If you're a real Christian, then you're on board with us so far. Therefore, there's only one surefire way of projecting an image of perfection to those around you: **doing life together.**

"Doing life together" is a term Paul used frequently in the New Testament that is perhaps better translated from the Greek as "just hanging out and doing whatever." Take a hobby that you enjoy, be it playing board games, shooting guns, or driving R/C cars around, call it fellowship, and presto, you're doing life together. So long as you have a favorite pastime, you're ready to redeem it for God's glory by labeling it as doing life together.*

Just check out the handy table below if you're ever in doubt that what you're doing counts as fellowship that grows you in your walk with Christ.

Activity	Does It Qualify as "Doing Life Together"?
Watching sports	Yes.
Texas Hold'em Tournament	Definitely doing life together.
Chillin' in Azeroth with your World of Warcraft clan	Oh, heck yeah!
Ladies' bunco night	You'd better believe it, sisters!
Bible study	Dangerously close to authentic connection—steer clear!

* Note that the activity only counts as doing life together when you do it with fellow believers. If done with non-Christians, you can call it evangelism and get even more spiritual credit! Awesome!

Looks just like doing whatever you want while getting spiritual points in the process, doesn't it? You're catching on.

Now, the secret to properly doing life around lesser Christians is to **redeem everything**. Redeeming everything means you're constantly relating whatever activity you and your buddies are doing to God and the gospel. This is a high-level move that can take some practice to get right, but it's totally worth learning how to do when you consider all the spiritual accolades you'll garner from your fellow Christians.

Let's say you're playing Settlers of Catan with some folks from church. While most people would just enjoy the game without trying to find some kind of connection to Jesus, *most people aren't as spiritual as you*. You need to show people how in tune with the things of God you are by drawing analogies and illustrations from absolutely everything that happens in the game to what Christ accomplished for His people on the cross.

For example, after making an ordinary resource trade in the game, you could say something like, "Man, isn't it cool how I selflessly traded you my last remaining lumber card so you could build a road? That's just like how the Lord traded the Lamb of God so He could make a way for us to connect with Him." Then hit everyone with one of your very best, ultra-spiritual looks of pensive meditation, drop your gaze to the floor, and take a deep breath, broadcasting your incredible connection with the things of God to these plebes who are just trying to enjoy a board game.

Pepper each round of play with these kinds of comments, and everyone around you will know just how saturated you are in the Word of God.*

Or take another seemingly secular activity like golf. To the untrained eye, golf is just a way to relax and enjoy God's creation while expressing creativity and using the bodies God gave us to honor Him. But to a superspiritual Christian like you, **golf is a springboard to loudly let everyone around you know how much more you love Jesus than they do.** Whenever you sink a putt, pause for a moment, tear up, and then say, "You know, sinking this left-to-right four-footer just reminded me of how, in a way, God gave us Jesus's perfect golf performance. And Jesus took our 48-over-par score as if it were His."

Man, that's good stuff.

And these ideas are just off the top of our heads. With some creative thinking, you can totally redeem all kinds of activities to the glory of God. And everyone around you will be able to glean some deep wisdom from your insights.

Christians who are still a lot more carnal than you might be annoyed by these kinds of comments, but they just need to be sanctified more thoroughly. Be patient and show them some grace. They're still works in progress. One day they'll be as holy as you are, and then they'll be able to make all the superdeep, gospel-centered observations that you can.

---

* When they stop inviting you over for game night, count it all joy. You're being persecuted for Jesus!

The key to the successful redemption of mundane activities is to never be content to just enjoy the good things God has given us. **Everything must be explicitly Christian** or else someone as devoted to Jesus as you are can't find any joy in it. Watching baseball games, going on a bike ride, playing *Super Smash Bros.*—all of these activities and more can become valuable rungs on the ladder to the summit of righteousness, as long as you're able to find some kind of connection to the gospel to assuage your guilt for having even a modicum of fun on this earth.

An advanced form of doing life together is to get the church to sponsor a hobby by labeling it a ministry. There's even the possibility of conning the church into buying all your expensive hobbyist equipment as a ministry expense! For example, if you're into guns, work your way up the ministry ladder until you're the head of the men's ministry. Then schedule multiple trips to a shooting range throughout the calendar year, and you're golden. *You can now buy guns and ammo on the church credit card!**

But we're getting ahead of ourselves. Before you can possibly work yourself up to that level of spiritual cunning and brilliance, you need to start with the basics, and that means **joining a small group** that meets at someone's home. You can only fly under the radar and hang out with Christians on an unofficial

---

* As a bonus, owning a gun nets you at least five hundred spiritual points (a thousand if combined with a concealed carry permit), as long as you're in a more conservative church. You get even more points if you become a member of the NRA and purchase a massive bumper sticker that says something like "Gun Control Means Using Both Hands."

basis for so long before the church will drag you into these smaller, more intimate gatherings.

Again, there's really no way around it, so just stiffen that upper lip and take care of business.

If you want to be a good Christian, a small group is an absolute must. Your new church should have come up with a really cool, relevant name for small groups. Something like Life Groups, Oikos Collectives, Dotcoms, or Hub Groups is ideal. The name should definitely mask the fact that the group is essentially a Bible study—after all, this is the twenty-first century, people.

The small group is an ingenious invention, first introduced by Martin Luther during the Protestant Reformation. According to legend, the great reformer asked four or five people from his *oikos* if they'd hang out, drink some beer, and listen to his wild-eyed rants about peasants and the pope and stuff from seven to nine every Friday night. Thus the very first small group was born.

Small groups allow your church to have tens of thousands of members but still make you feel as if you actually know people at the church. The church gets all the perks of having a massive operating budget and sprawling campus, but it doesn't actually have to disciple people or foster real connections on Sunday mornings. It's a real lifesaver for the megachurch pastor who no longer has to make an effort to get to know all the lesser members of the body of Christ.

When you arrive at your first small group meeting (early, of course), the host family will warmly greet you and invite you to make yourself at home. **We recommend an immediate inspection of the premises to ensure the place is going to meet your lofty standards.** Don't worry, they'll be expecting this. March straight over to the fridge and scour that puppy high and low to make sure they don't have any alcohol. If they're crafty (pun!), they'll have hidden any beer or wine high up on a shelf in the garage. So feel free to give yourself a tour of the home as you search every nook and cranny for the slightest evidence that they treat themselves to the devil's drink on occasion. If you find so much as a small plastic bottle of cooking wine, excuse yourself and leave at once. Your Christian perfection is at stake here.

Your next stop should be their movie shelf, where you can make passive-aggressive comments about the kinds of secular movies they own: "Oh, you own every season of *Game of Thrones*? Could you give me directions to a small group nearby that actually loves Jesus?" Perfect Christians never miss an opportunity to judge other Christians on issues of conscience, and dropping some scathing remarks about their movie collection is a moment God prepared before the creation of the world for you to get a leg up on those spiritual failures.

After you've demonstrated your superiority to the small group's hosts, the slightly-less-spiritual members will eventually arrive, and you'll finally be able to get down to business.

Your church's small group meetings are the ideal place to show off your spiritual muscles and assert your superior spiritual acumen in front of your fellow churchgoers.

To conduct yourself properly in a small group, **answer every question the group leader asks**. Every one. Even if you have no idea what the answer is, don't let on that you're completely clueless. Just raise your hand and start talking about absolutely anything at all. Lead the group off onto as many completely unrelated rabbit trails as possible. When the group leader corrects you or suggests that your exegesis of *Battlestar Galactica*'s awful ending to season four just isn't relevant right now, boldly declare that his take on the Bible passage you're discussing is only *his* interpretation.

If you want to take this maneuver to the next level, seize the initiative and **question everything the group leader says**. Shake your head, furrow your brow, and write furiously in the margins of your Bible whenever he or anyone else makes a truth claim. When someone takes the bait and asks you what's the matter, just say, "Oh, nothing. It's just that when I was young and naive, I used to think that way too. But if that's where God has you on your journey right now, that's fine too, I guess."

Let no statement, no matter how innocuous, pass without weighing in. Those around you can really benefit from your discernment and wisdom as you mercilessly thrash them with your feigned knowledge of the Scriptures.

Sample Small Group Conversation

SMALL GROUP LEADER: So it's pretty cool here that Paul shows how God is both just and the justifier of His people through His display of righteousness on the cross. Does anyone have any questions about that?

YOU: Yeah, I do. I mean, your interpretation is, shall we say, interesting. But I think it's really about how we shouldn't judge people for their lifestyle choices. If you really knew your Bible, you'd know that this passage means "judge not."

SMALL GROUP LEADER: Where is that in the text?

YOU: Whoa, bro. There you go again with being judgmental. I just have a burning conviction in my heart telling me that the text means "don't judge people." But if your interpretation is right for you, then that's cool, man, as long as you're okay with being a fundamentalist.

By this point, the rest of the small group should be nodding in approval, in awe of your biblical knowledge and how full you are of the love of Christ. You can capitalize on this on the spot by group-texting all of them a link to your blog, where they can read more of your innovative, edgy takes on Christianity. Heck, if you play your cards right, you might even be able to stage a mutiny against the small group leader and start your own ultra-exclusive small group for only superspiritual Christians.

But for now, when the study finally comes to an end, after you've stretched it out with all your holy-sounding interjections, it'll be time to close in prayer.

This might sound boring on the surface, but hear us out: **praying among other Christians is an awesome way to grow in perceived righteousness.** Here are a few simple tricks to help you pray in public.

Praying with Power

- **Use the phrase "Father God" like it's going out of style.** After all, God might forget that you're addressing Him if you don't keep dropping "Father God" in there. Plus, it just sounds *super*-righteous. Think of every "Father God" as a spiritual point, and stack those babies up.

- **Say "just" every other word.** This communicates to the Christians around you that you speak their language. Using the word "just" is one of the signs of a true believer, according to the New Testament, so sprinkling the word throughout your prayer will have the added benefit of reaffirming your assurance of salvation. Ninety percent of any good prayer is comprised of the three words "just," "Father," and "God."

- **Take on a Puritan persona throughout your prayer.**
  You can either memorize old Puritan prayers or just
  mimic their ultraholy vocabulary. Above all else,
  you don't just want to sound like a laid-back dude
  talking to his heavenly Father. Nope. You want to
  impress God with thy thees and thous.

- **Pray for almost three hours so everyone sees how
  holy you are.** Muttering something about your
  gratitude to Jesus for thirty seconds is no good.
  A minimum of three hours of prayer will definitely
  get you to the next rung on the ladder of holiness.

- **Correct other people's prayers.** If the girl who prays
  before you asks for healing for her grandmother,
  make sure you say something like, "Father God,
  while healing for Jane's grandmother would be
  nice, I'd like to ask for something more: for You
  to be glorified in whatever outcome You see fit."
  Constantly one-upping your fellow believers in
  holiness is a foundational element of solid cor-
  porate prayer.

- **Pray two or three times just to keep the group on
  their toes.** Just when everyone thinks the prayer
  circle is done, jump in there again with another few
  hours of prayer. Wait until everyone else starts to
  open their eyes and sit up straight, and then just
  keep right on going with something like, "And

Father God, we just want to lift up before you now the people in Uganda, and just, also Father God, just the people in Zimbabwe, and also Father God . . ."

- **Use big, bibley words, even if you don't understand them.** We'll let you in on a little secret: the rumor from on high is that God doesn't hear prayers that don't use phrases like "imputed righteousness," "penal substitutionary atonement," and "the eternal submission of the Son." So don't be afraid to drop the J-bomb (justification), the H-bomb (hamartiology), or even the rare M-bomb (Melchizedekian priesthood). If you don't know what these things mean, don't worry, because nobody else does either.

Of course, this all assumes you're regularly attending a small group in the first place. While you want to join such a group in order to appear spiritual, you also want to **minimize your attendance** so your spirituality points go up while you do absolutely nothing. It's a careful balancing act.

As the start time for the small group meeting looms closer and closer each week, begin looking for possible excuses to miss it. Is there the faintest outline of a cloud on the horizon? Say you're going to stay home due to the impending inclement weather. Want to go to a midweek sporting event instead? Say you're taking a break this week in order to "spend some time with the Lord" (uttering a prayer for your favorite baseball team at the game totally counts!). The key is to come up with the most spiritual-sounding justifications to avoid genuine connection while still blessing the group with your presence on occasion to keep up appearances.

Be careful, however. By actually getting up close and personal with other Christians, who are undoubtedly much further from Christlikeness than you are, you run the risk of making an actual friend who wants to hang out or grab a coffee or even meet up for discipleship. You attend group one too many times this year, and someone is inevitably going to break into the discipleship danger zone.

While this is a very serious situation, as it can cause your carefully constructed facade of Christianity to come crumbling down, you can leverage it to your advantage and come out looking even holier than before.

Don't worry! We're here to help you navigate these tricky waters. If you do ever end up getting dragged to coffee, dinner, or—shudder—a one-on-one Bible study with a friend from church, do not panic. We can help you with that.

It is of the utmost importance that you **never allow any conversations to go beyond surface level**. Keep your fellow believers at arm's length. You must prevent any kind of genuine connection at any cost.

A large part of this will be comprised of using the right Christian buzzwords and insider language to clue them in that everything is totally fine in your life.

We'll let you in on an insider secret: gaining the praise and accolades of your Christian friends isn't so much about *walking the walk* as it is *talking the talk*.

Paul reiterates this idea in his letter to the church at Ephesus: "Let no corrupting talk come out of your mouths, but only such as is good for building up, as fits the occasion, that it may give grace to those who hear" (Ephesians 4:29, ESV). The Bible also tells us that we ought to let our speech be "full of grace, seasoned with salt" so we will know how to answer those who oppose us (Colossians 4:6). Keeping an eye on our speech is important for Christians, because we know that we will give an account for "every careless word" that we speak (Matthew 12:36).

The proper application of these verses and others like them is that you should **try really hard to sound spiritual in your interactions with other Christians.**

Therefore, whether you're dealing with Christians from your superawesome you-centric church in a small group setting or a one-on-one environment, you're going to want to learn the language of true disciples: **Christianese.**

Christianese is an ancient dialect of English that traces its roots all the way back to the 1950s. It's a secret language known only to the superspiritual. When you can successfully carry on a full conversation in Christianese, you'll know you have at long last entered the upper echelons of Christian spirituality.

To get you started, turn the page for a helpful translation guide containing some popular Christianese phrases.

Christianese Phrase	English Translation
"I'll keep that in prayer, brother."	"I have no intentions of praying for you. In fact, I've already forgotten what it is you were going on about. Why are you still talking?"
"Lord willing."	"I'm gonna do it whether the Lord wants me to or not, but I want to sound like I'm trusting God in this situation."
"Bless her heart!"	"We are so much holier than that spiritual failure, it's incredible."
"I'm just really focusing on dating God right now."	"I'm not interested in you, but I don't want to hurt your feelings, so I'm gonna play the God card."
"I'd love to have you over for some fellowship soon."	"I run a home-based business and I'm going to try to sell you stuff for the duration of our relationship."

Christianese Phrase	English Translation
"I just don't really feel called to that ministry opportunity."	"That ministry sounds suspiciously like work and involves little to no glory or acclaim, so I'll wait for something a little more glamorous before I'll hear the Lord's still small voice calling me to serve."
"I'm just waiting on the Lord right now."	"I am still living with my parents."
"I really feel like this is God's will for my life."	"I'm sick of people pointing out all the glaringly obvious flaws in my life plan, so I'll just slap the handy 'God's will' label on it to silence the wisdom of my critics."
"We just invite your presence into this place, now, Father God."	"None of you heathens were clapping during that last song. Get it together, people."

Memorize lots of bibley-sounding phrases, and season your conversations with them liberally. The perfect Christian will sound like a walking, talking Bible dictionary, effortlessly weaving totally meaningless words and phrases to accomplish the underlying purpose of impressing all his believing friends.

While we could go on and on coaching you on all the ins and outs of keeping up appearances among your brothers and sisters in Christ, we'll mention a final and essential element of doing life together: **select a really holy-looking Bible to carry around.**

We'll deal with the appropriate Bible translation a little later on. For now, the most important thing is to choose a **massive, ornate Bible.** We're talking one that's so heavy you need a caddy to carry it around for you. It definitely needs to have the words "Study Bible" embossed in gold on the cover, preferably the Ryrie, MacArthur, or Reformation varieties for maximum impact on those watching you. It should also have your name stamped on the cover. Not only will your Bible be returned to you if it gets misplaced, but a name imprinted in gold is as good as getting your name written in the Lamb's Book of Life.

It's total assurance of salvation without having to worry about looking for the fruit of the Spirit in your life.

Make sure to bring your Bible to every church event, even ones that don't seem to require an expensive study Bible the size of a compact car. A Bible app on your phone will not do. Well, maybe for those spiritual weaklings around you. But if you do end up needing to look up a verse, how will people know you're reading the Bible and not just knocking out a few levels in the latest mobile game?

For you, O great Christian, bringing your Bible to even the most secular-sounding events lets everyone know that it's spiritual go time. It is *on* like *Donkey Kong* whenever you're around. It doesn't matter if you're going to a church-sponsored baseball game, barbecue, or 5K run. Like a trusted sidekick, your largest, fanciest study Bible should be with you at all times.

Now, friend, you have mastered the art of doing life together. Let's check in with the Holiness Tracker and see how you're doing.

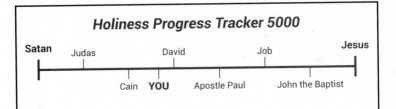

Holiness Progress Tracker 5000

Satan   Judas   David   Job   Jesus

Cain   **YOU**   Apostle Paul   John the Baptist

Whaaaaaat?! You're nearing David himself, the man after God's own heart! You're still a way off from the truly Christlike people, but we've gotta say, we didn't really expect this kind of a performance out of you. You're amazing!

SERVING IN CHURCH WITHOUT EVER LIFTING A FINGER

Ask not what you can do for your church. Ask what your church can do for you.

—Dietrich Bonhoeffer

We hope you've joined a church that is more concerned with throwing wild parties and entertainment extravaganzas than it is with doing actual ministry. If your church cares about the New Testament model at all, it's throwing a lot more glow-stick raves and monster-truck rallies than it is homeless outreaches and evangelism nights. Should the monster-truck-rally-to-homeless-outreach ratio be out of whack, it's time for you to go back and reread chapter 1. There's no use in continuing down the path of holiness if you're in a church that's going to keep bringing you down with discipleship, ministry opportunities, and the like.

During the rare occasions when your exciting you-centered church does actual ministry, **your primary goal is, at all costs, to avoid lifting a finger.** Make no mistake, now that you've joined up with a church and are plugged in with a small group, church leadership is going to go after you *hard* to force you to sign up for a ministry or volunteer at some lame outreach event. Your pastor smells volunteer blood in the water every time you walk by.

Let's get biblical for a moment. The only thing Jesus ever said about serving in the church was recorded in Matthew 11:30: "My yoke is easy and my burden is light." As Christians, therefore, our solemn duty is to hang back and let everyone else do the work.*

If you're taking this Christianity thing seriously, then, your job is to come up with **any excuse necessary** to get yourself off the hook of serving the body of Christ.

The sinister free-time-destroying call to ministry comes in many forms. Your church might passive-aggressively place ministry sign-up forms in the lobbies, which are easy enough to avoid by just pretending you don't see them. Give them a wide berth, as though they're deadly land mines. Sometimes, if they get desperate for volunteers, they'll guilt-trip the whole congregation with an announcement that they really need more people to step up to watch the two- and three-year-olds, visit a convalescent home, or something else totally lame like that. These are slightly tougher to navigate, so you'll need to be on top of your eye-contact avoidance game to make it through

---

* This is definitely the correct interpretation of this verse. We talked to dozens of prominent Bible scholars, and they all agreed, so there's no need for you to go looking into it yourself. We got you, fam.

unscathed. Pretend you're concentrating really hard on your Bible, fake that you're in a deep time of meditative prayer, or jump up with a spontaneous word of prophecy in an angelic tongue. Get creative here—absolutely any technique to get out of dull ministry work is fair game.

The worst-case scenario is that the pastor approaches you as you make a beeline for your car after the service and straight up, point-blank asks you to help out once in a while. Don't bother with the biblical explanation of why you're opposed to pitching in—your scriptural acumen will intimidate him and make him defensive.

Instead, a nearly ironclad excuse that works in this dangerous situation is to say that you **just don't feel called to help out at your church.** Commit the following to memory and use them whenever necessary: "I don't feel called," "I don't believe the Lord is leading me," "I'm not feeling led down that path." These are powerful trump cards you should keep at the ready for times like this.

Here is a sample conversation to help you the next time the pastor rudely asks you to volunteer, no matter how small the commitment may seem:

PASTOR: Hey, man. I noticed you're really gifted with loving on people. I think it'd be a big blessing for you and for the church if you'd serve on the prayer team, even if it's just fifteen minutes every other month.

YOU: That sounds amazing, my brother in Christ, and I'd really like to press in on that with you. But you know, I just don't really feel called to help out in that way.

PASTOR: Oh, why not?

YOU: Well, here's the thing, brother—God just hasn't put it on my heart. I don't feel a mystical burning sensation in my bowels when I think about volunteering to gather with other Christians and briefly pray for the life of the church.

PASTOR: Oh, all right then. Uh, I guess that makes sense. Is there some other way you do feel God calling you to serve the body of Christ?

YOU: That's a great question, pastor. But I want to be careful not to do anything that's outside the will of God, so I'm really going to have to keep that in prayer for the next several years before I can commit to anything.

PASTOR: Sounds good.*

As shown in the example above, if the pastor ever corners you and you run out of excuses, just say you're going to keep it in prayer. (Don't actually pray about it, of course. God might

---

* Run, don't walk, away from the conversation at the first possible moment. Jump in your car and floor it. Hanging around the church grounds too long after the service is unwise, as you'll inevitably get asked time and again to serve in various ministries.

actually convict you of the need for you to love your fellow Christians, which would be unbiblical.) This shuts the pastor down right at the start, and it has the added benefit of making you sound spiritual, and you still haven't even lifted a finger! It's like getting something for nothing. "Keeping it in prayer" is an excellent little Jedi mind trick to convince people you're really close to the Lord and to make sure no one ever catches on that you've never once helped out at the church.

As we've established from the beginning, the church is here to meet *your* needs, not the other way around. Theologians call this "you-centered ministry," and it's totally biblical. Trust us on that. **Make sure you and your church never lose sight of that God-ordained priority**.

So, hey, why not put your newly honed volunteer-avoidance skills to the test right away? If your church is in the Baptist or Methodist tradition, there's probably a potluck scheduled for this coming Sunday. This is a great opportunity for you to be served by other people at church while doing very little work yourself.

Christ left three ordinances for the local church: baptism, the Lord's Supper, and the **potluck**. The latter is a sacred tradition, thousands of years old. In fact, biblical scholars now believe Christ's final Passover supper with His disciples was a potluck, with each of the disciples offering to bring a different hot dish for everyone to enjoy.*

---

* According to the latest research, Judas Iscariot brought Jell-O filled with questionable fruit pieces.

At the potluck, everyone contributes a plate of tasty food, and then all attendees get to enjoy a little bit of whatever their hearts desire. Studies have shown that attending potlucks and consuming thousands of calories of melted cheese, fried chicken, and questionably cooked meat is almost guaranteed to prolong your life by a good thirty or forty years. So you're going to want to jump right in with both feet and do life together, potluck-style. You do care about your health, don't you?

Your goal at the potluck is to enjoy as much food as possible while providing the absolute minimum contribution yourself. Slip in undetected and drop a twenty-five-pack of store-brand napkins on the table or offer to carry some clueless grandma's contribution into the fellowship hall and then pretend you made that crispy chicken casserole from scratch while she's still hobbling in from her Cadillac with her walker.

Alternatively, do the really spiritual thing and bring **nothing at all**. You tithe to the church, don't you? Why are they asking you to give a penny more than the customary 2 percent? They're greedy, that's why. All they care about is money, or else they'd let you have everything for free.

But just because you didn't bring much doesn't mean you don't get to gorge yourself swollen on the glorious mountain of casseroles. No sir or madam! You eat as though you're on death row. Bring a large purse or man-bag and just scrape a few generous helpings of every last hot dish on the communal table right on in there. Pack a thermos and pour all the store-brand two-liter bottles of soda someone else paid for in it so you can enjoy their generic goodness at home. You've gotta get your tithe's worth.

The potluck is just a proving ground, your own personal Hunger Games, to see if you're the very best at slacking off and leeching off others' hard labor.

Once you're sneaking into the biweekly potluck like a pro, you're ready to ascend to the next plateau of greatness by **figuring out what your spiritual gift is.**

A spiritual gift is a unique blend of supernaturally bestowed talents and passions granted to everyone who believes in Jesus. For instance, Moses had the spiritual gift of getting really mad and breaking stuff. Samson had the spiritual gift of growing a really dope beard. And Peter had the spiritual gift of saying the exact wrong thing at the exact wrong time.

We'll be forthright with you: some spiritual gifts are way better than others. Some are the spiritual equivalent of *The Dark Knight* trilogy while others are the *Batman & Robin* of spiritual gifts. To discern which one God has infused you with, start by perusing the list of spiritual gifts on the next page.

Carefully look over this list, pray for a couple seconds if you feel like it, and then choose the one that sounds the best to you. Congratulations! That's your new spiritual gift!

Don't really worry about what you're actually good at. Just choose the one that's most beneficial for you. If you don't

Spiritual Gift	Description	Awesomeness Level
Tongues	Babbling incoherently and calling it a private prayer language.	**8/10** — You're so much better than those carnal Christians who never got a second blessing! If they even *are* Christians.
Teaching	The supernatural ability to preach from a MacBook Pro sitting on a sleek, modern café table. Includes ability to make hilarious jokes every other sentence and tell heartwarming anecdotes.	**11/10** — You are literally the center of attention while teaching. And people will tell you how awesome you are all the time. It's definitely the best spiritual gift of them all.
Hospitality	Allows you to bake casseroles for people and do stuff for them or something.	**0/10** — You don't get much praise for this one, so steer clear.
Peddling the gospel for boatloads of money	Just turn on TBN and mimic what those guys do, and you'll know if you have the right stuff for this spiritual gift!	**9/10** — You get lots of money and fame. The only downside is there's a small chance you go to prison for tax evasion.

actually possess the gift you've chosen, don't worry. Take a bit of wisdom from Proverbs and "fake it 'til you make it."

Now, look, if you happen to fail at deflecting your pastor's requests to serve, or if your pastor is just a bulldog who won't take no for an answer, then take our advice and **join a ministry** to get the guy off your back.

Don't worry, the goal stays the same—you still won't be lifting a finger. But now you'll get credit for saying you serve in a church ministry. Score!

Let's take a tour of some of the most common ministry areas most churches have. We'll provide an in-depth analysis of each in order to help you select the one that will bring you the most glory while requiring the least effort.

- **Tech Ministry:** Volunteering in the tech ministry means you've given up on becoming a prominent Christian of whom people will be talking about for years to come. Not one person will even know you exist. In fact, the only time anyone will ever look at you is when you bungle a worship slide on Sunday morning or if one of the mics stops working. Then the entire congregation will know just how much of a failure you are.

   This ministry also requires quite a bit of technical knowledge, so the work-to-glory ratio is really out of whack. We'd recommend a hard pass on anything related to the audiovisual ministry.

- **Worship Ministry**: Worship ministry is pretty great. You get to pretend you're a real rock star, but you only need a fraction of the talent. Only bother to apply if you're ridiculously attractive or else your modest looks will distract people from their worship of God and their awestruck adoration of the worship band.

  If your worship band's music is just above mediocre, there's a chance you'll get picked up by a major contemporary Christian record label, and then you'll be swimming in fame and fortune. So if you've got the looks, the designer wardrobe, and the modest guitar chord repertoire, you ought to consider this one.

- **Youth Ministry**: There are only two kinds of people who volunteer for youth ministry: self-loathing masochists and aspiring pastors who are just doing their time until they're ready for *actual* ministry. You do, however, get lots of free pizza, soda, and video game time, so it's not all bad. Just remember that you'll have to supplement your less-than-minimum-wage income with panhandling or running a massive drug-dealing empire to make rent each month.

- **Men's Ministry**: A church's pastor to men is usually just a pastor who isn't cool enough to be the main dude, like those local punk bands at the Vans

Warped Tour who play on the side stage. He could also be a senior pastor who was edged out of the pulpit after reaching the ancient age of thirty-nine. The silver lining with men's ministry is that you get to shoot a lot of stuff, roll around in the mud, and use phrases like "biblical manhood" to package it as real Christian ministry. Neat!

- **Women's Ministry**: Women's ministry is reserved for women who are gifted in teaching but aren't allowed to use their gifting anywhere else. They get to throw lots of tea parties, spa nights, and Avon makeup sales pitches cleverly disguised as Bible studies. While women's ministry is almost as lame as children's ministry, it's as good as you can hope for, ladies. So take what you can get.

- **Children's Ministry**: Children's ministry is super-lame. You get very little glory and you're dealing with harebrained kids who aren't gonna remember what you're talking about five minutes later, let alone by the time they get home (kind of like pastoring adults, but even more so). You'll serve lots of Goldfish crackers and punch and come home covered in peculiar substances. We suppose you could do this for the satisfaction of doing it or to invest in the future generation of believers, but really it's just far too much work to be worth it.

- **Nursery:** Same as children's ministry above but with more diaper changing and lots of drooling. It's basically a dungeon of tears and poop. Serving in the nursery is the bottom of the totem pole.

As you select the ministry that's right for you, consider elements like **how much of your free time it will suck up, how much glory you will get for your work,** and **how well it pays.** With a little prayer and meditation, God will surely lead you to the ministry that fits you like a nice cashmere sweater and also earns you the praise of man.

No matter what ministry you serve in, remember the golden rule: **let everyone else do all the heavy lifting.** We mean this literally. If the potluck is wrapping up and people are tearing down tables and chairs, stand off to the side and engage in spiritual conversations about the things of God. Should someone dare approach you and ask if you'd lend a hand, hit 'em with a zinger like, "Oh, sorry. I was just over here discussing the gospel-centered gospel with a brother in the Lord. I didn't realize you didn't care about Jesus at all."

Another approach would be to tell them your spiritual gift is *encouragement* rather than actually working. Then give 'em a pat on the back and say, "Nice job, buddy. I'm really impressed with your servant's heart." You look holy and they do all the labor. It's a win-win.

This is fundamental, people. If church really is all about you (see chapter 1), then the pastor and the rest of the hundreds of people on the church staff should be waiting on you hand and foot, not asking you to do a bunch of lame stuff.

Doesn't it feel good to be the king of the hill at your church? Getting all the glory while putting in minimal effort? Speaking from experience, we can say there's no greater joy in the world, no matter what John Piper says.

Let's check in with the tracker and see how well you're doing.

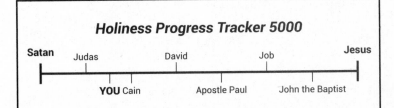

Holiness Progress Tracker 5000

Satan — Judas — YOU / Cain — David — Apostle Paul — Job — John the Baptist — Jesus

Wait, what? You backslid? Ugh.

You must have gone out and done actual ministry without letting everyone else do all the difficult, unglamorous work. What were you thinking?

You'd better get back on track if you ever want to achieve perfection. Stop messing around. We've got work to do!

Five

LOOKING REALLY SPIRITUAL ONLINE

If a man reads his Bible but fails to post pictures of it on the Internet, did it really happen?

—Chinese proverb, circa 2500 BC

So far we've addressed your spiritual maturity solely in the context of the local church. Holiness begins there as you endeavor to make a name for yourself as the most righteous person in your congregation. You'll only grow more mature in your walk with Jesus if you're plugged into the lifeblood of the body of Christ, where you can use your God-given talents and spiritual gifts for your glory.*

But if you truly desire to become perfect, you'll need to kick it up a notch. **You must learn how to broadcast your spiritual achievements for all to see by using the power of the**

---

* We have no idea why God designed the Christian life this way. We really wish He had taken our input, because we totally would have had much better ideas, like just letting people do the Christian life on their own or attending church online. Bush-league, God. Real bush-league.

Internet. What's the use of being a perfect Christian if you can't tell everyone about it? Exactly!

During the Sermon on the Mount, Jesus talked about this very concept:

> Be careful not to do your "acts of righteousness" before men, to be seen by them. If you do, you will have no reward from your Father in heaven.
>
> So when you give to the needy, do not announce it with trumpets, as the hypocrites do in the synagogues and on the streets, to be honored by men. I tell you the truth, they have received their reward in full. But when you give to the needy, do not let your left hand know what your right hand is doing, so that your giving may be in secret. Then your Father, who sees what is done in secret, will reward you.
>
> And when you pray, do not be like the hypocrites, for they love to pray standing in the synagogues and on the street corners to be seen by men. I tell you the truth, they have received their reward in full. But when you pray, go into your room, close the door and pray to your Father, who is unseen. Then your Father, who sees what is done in secret, will reward you. And when you pray, do not keep on babbling like pagans, for they think they will be heard because of their many words. Do

not be like them, for your Father knows what you need before you ask him. (Matthew 6:1–8)

The Lord is very clear here: **any acts of charity or times of prayer aren't to be advertised to the world using trumpets or many spiritual-sounding words in the synagogue.** Waltzing right into the Jewish place of worship and sounding the horn of your own spirituality would just be self-centered and would show a real lack of humility. And if there's anyone who doesn't lack humility, it's you, brave Christian.

Luckily, Jesus didn't realize that He was leaving a massive loophole open for us: He didn't say a single thing about taking pictures of your prayer times and sharing them on social media. Seriously. Go back and read it again. As long as you don't use a trumpet or talk about it loudly in a first-century synagogue, it's totally biblical!

Isn't exegesis* awesome?

The Internet is so much better than a trumpet anyway. In ancient Israel, if you wanted other believers to see how holy you were, you'd need to use those trumpets, which Jesus condemned, or make your way into the synagogue to just destroy the religious leaders with your spiritual knowledge of the Scriptures.

---

* We don't know what that means, either. But it sure sounds cool!

The catch is you actually had to spend a lifetime studying the Word of God if you wanted to be regarded well in the Jewish community. **LOL!**

Years of study? Whole decades committed to poring over God's Word? Boooooooriiiing! As you can imagine, it was hard work earning any ancient holiness points at all! But now the Internet lets you display your great piety for all to see, racking up tons of treasure in heaven for yourself. And you don't even need to read the text: you just need to get a really good filtered shot of an open Bible, and you're golden. And while people in Jesus's day, if they were lucky, could only expect for their good deeds to be seen by no more than maybe a few hundred people, your righteousness has serious potential to go viral and be seen by millions! Praise the Lord!

But none of this will happen if you don't spend time in serious prayer.

So to begin to revitalize your prayer life, **you need to learn the biblical practice of posting pictures of yourself during your quiet times with Jesus to every social media channel available.** A recent study found a strong correlation between publishing pictures of one's personal devotions and a vibrant spiritual life. Those who posted several dozen pictures per devotional time were found to be 428 percent holier than those who rarely or never posted pictures of themselves next to an open Bible and a hot cup of coffee.

If you really desire to be perfect, it's time to get posting!

But not just any lame snapshot will do. You want an attention-grabbing photo. You want your quiet time to go viral! Luckily, you're reading a book written by the experts. **For high-quality spiritual pictures of your open Bible, just remember the acronym CHAFF.**

- **C—COFFEE**: Make sure you get a cup of tasty joe in your picture. True Christians study the Word of God with a mug of artisan, fair-trade, non-GMO, gluten-free, cage-free, nonalcoholic coffee. Taking the picture while at a coffee shop even shows that you don't care if the world knows you're a Jesus freak. Bonus points, baby!

- **H—HASHTAGS**: Hashtag that sucker for maximum reach. We recommend hashtags like #blessed, #amen, #holy, #iambetterthanyou, and #lookeveryoneimreadingmyBible to ensure your personal time of communion with God through His Word goes viral.

- **A—AUDIENCE**: Don't forget that you're doing this for an audience of one *million*. Share that picture on *all* your social networks, not just one. And if you don't get a boatload of engagement and attention the first time, don't be afraid to repost it throughout the day. You could even tag some big-name Christian celebrities and pray to the Lord above that one of them retweets it for maximum exposure. Best-case scenario: your artsy picture of your communion with the Lord Most High gets spotted by Ellen, and you get to appear on a daytime talk show!

F—FILTER: A plain-Jane picture of an open Bible never got anyone on the express lane to heaven. You need to use filters to make the image appear deep and spiritual. Apply an authentic vintage look, and you can be sure you'll get a like from Jesus Himself.

F—FAT: As in the size of your Bible. Use a fat, thick, leather-bound study Bible. Make sure to get the gold-embossed title on the spine in the picture, so everyone knows you read your MacArthur Study Bible regularly. Weather your Bible before the shot, too, to give it a worn, distressed look.

Posting pictures of yourself in deep fellowship with the Lord is just one way to grow in your faith online.

Another time-tested method is to **get involved in bitter arguments with people from all faith traditions and backgrounds every day.**

It's well known that the majority of converts to Christianity came to accept Jesus as their Lord and Savior after a Christian friend just went nuclear on them online. Psychology experts believe that the more you use derogatory terms to refer to other religions and nonbelievers, the more attractive your belief system appears. It may not make sense when you first think about it, but trust us, it's science.

So make sure not to let a single post that contains an opinion even slightly different from your own pass you by. Remember, a truly perfect Christian life is all focused on you alone, so if someone goes against your opinions, it's your duty to correct them. After all, someone's eternal destiny could depend on it. We're not just talking about theological arguments, either—make every single minor issue a hill to die on. For example, if someone expresses their preference for a single-column Bible, but you prefer a double-column version, dig your heels in and stay up late into the night flaming that person. Question their salvation at every turn, because they clearly have no idea what they're talking about.

Even arguments with other Christians could be noticed by nonbelievers and result in their accepting Christ as they see how much of a debate whiz you are. If you see something, say something. If someone is wrong about even a seemingly minor issue, rip right into them.

Let's get you started. Here are some sample comments you might consider posting on your friend's social media updates.

Friend's Update	Your Response
Sometimes I'm just not sure if God is there for me.	Did you know the Bible calls atheists "fools"? You're obviously a total moron.
"For God so loved the world that he gave his one and only Son, that whoever believes in him shall not perish but have eternal life." John 3:16 NIV <3 <3 <3	The NIV is a satanic Bible translation and you are going to hell.
10 years ago today I received Christ and was born again. Praise God for His mercy and love!	Regeneration precedes faith, heretic! Repent!
Little Johnny won his T-ball game today! Woo-hoo!	You allow your family to participate in sports on Sundays??? WOW... some people. SMH

Not only will your online arguments get people saved, but they're also essential to your own spiritual health. All the great Christians of centuries past found that they were closest to God when just absolutely blasting people on Facebook. It's been said that the famed Puritan preacher Jonathan Edwards actually wrote his famous sermon "Sinners in the Hands of an Angry God" on his MacBook while switching back and forth between his message prep time and totally owning an atheist on Facebook. Scholars also believe the long-lost letters of Paul to Corinth were actually long-winded, barely coherent rants in which he totally slammed a dude who slightly disagreed with him on major issues like women in ministry and the five points of Calvinism.

You do want to be like Jonathan Edwards and the apostle Paul, don't you? If not, we might be wasting our time with you, so go ahead and pass this book on to a friend or family member who possesses the divine spark that you clearly lack.

Of course, all your spiritual activity online may go to waste if you fail to present yourself in the right way in the first place. We're talking about an important spiritual discipline called **inflating your importance in your online profiles**. It's time to toot your own horn. (Again, not those temple trumpets Jesus was talking about. This is a totally different thing.)

We've got a few suggestions and some humble descriptors for your online profiles: speaker, writer, sojourner, thought leader, most supreme excellent Bible ninja, his holiness, highly favored child of the King, social justice warrior, humblessed.

And here are some other great tips:

- **Profile picture.** Use the portrait of a Reformer like John Calvin or Martin Luther to show your vast knowledge of church history figures. The other acceptable option is a very professional-looking close-up with a dark, dramatic gradient background that just shouts "I'm important!" You can even choose a profile overlay filter highlighting a political cause, signaling your lofty sense of virtue to your friends.

- **Cover/background image.** Display an open Bible with tons of highlighting. If you've never opened your Bible, don't worry. You can search for an image of one online and pretend it's yours.
- **Description.** Write lots of spiritual-sounding labels for yourself. Spin any fault or shortcoming into an advantage, like you're filling out a résumé for a highly competitive job.
- **Interests.** List Christian bands, Christian books, Christian causes, and Christian leaders as your only interests. Don't let any secular personalities creep into your interest lists, no matter how innocuous they may seem. Can light have any fellowship with darkness? No? Then you can't follow Walmart on Facebook, because Walmart isn't Christian!

Once your profile is up to snuff, spend every waking moment projecting an aura of perfection to your rapidly growing army of loyal followers.

Let's say you want to upload a picture of your kids so people will know what a godly parent you are. Should you just snap a pic and let people see how imperfect your life really is? *May it never be!* First, you'll need to spend hours cleaning your house so it looks like you've got everything under control.

Then, carefully stage the photo so the children are doing something hilarious or ultraspiritual. **As many shots as it takes.** Next, make up something cute that one of them said, even if all they're really saying is, "Mom, can I please go upstairs and play *Minecraft* now? I'm bored." Then revel in your shower of likes and heart emojis.

You might even consider turning some of your mundane quotes into image macros. Whenever you make a stale observation like "Today is not yesterday, nor is it tomorrow" or "I could really use a taco right now" or anything, really, just upload a picture of your face superimposed on a mountain range or a sunset on the beach. Then, share that thing like it's going out of style so others can profit from your words of wisdom and in turn make you look really good. For example, something like this would be an instant hit:

Also, when you're browsing your favorite social network, you may come across a picture of a pasty-white Jesus who looks as though He gets a $400 cut and color three times a week. This image of the Savior will be accompanied by a caption that says something like "1 share = 1 amen. 1 ignore = 1 Satan." Obviously, you need to like, share, and leave a comment like "Amen!" accompanied by a "blessed" hashtag. How will Jesus—and more important, your army of followers—know you love Jesus unless you're constantly liking pictures of Him on Facebook?

And this should go without saying, but for the love of all that is holy, **don't forget to "check in" at church every time you attend**. A representative for heaven recently confirmed that every time you check in at church on Facebook, you're earning yourself the equivalent of $10,000 in heavenly treasure to spend in the afterlife. And to earn some bonus heaven bucks, add a few praying-hands emojis to kick-start your eternal retirement fund. Checking in at church doesn't just pay off in the final state, however; it helps you accomplish your goal of alerting everyone on earth to the shining brilliance of your holiness.

You see, the underlying mission in your interactions with others online, whether Christians or heathens, is to **project an image of perfection**. Every post, every photo, every video, every status update should be done with this ultimate purpose in mind: to glorify yourself by conforming to cultural Christian standards in all things. Eternity is at stake here, folks! You don't have time to mess around.

Never let on that you're normal—or mortal.

Because you're not.

You're on your way to being a *perfect Christian*. Check it out.

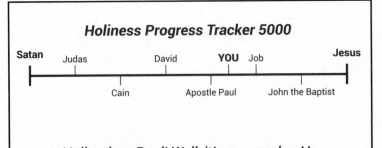

Holiness Progress Tracker 5000

Satan   Judas   David   **YOU** Job   **Jesus**
         Cain   Apostle Paul   John the Baptist

Holier than Paul! Well, it's no wonder. He didn't have the Internet to help him out! You're really getting the hang of this. Do a little fist pump in your own honor.

Six

STRIVING FOR PERSONAL PERFECTION

Before you drink that beer, you've gotta ask yourself one question: "Do I feel lucky?" Well, do ya, punk?

—Billy Graham

According to theologians, sanctification is defined as the spiritual process whereby Christians are conformed more and more into the image of Christ. While we are justified freely by His grace and granted Christ's righteousness the moment we believe, the journey toward Christlikeness on this earth is often a long, slow, painful one.

Sounds terrible, right? It's a real downer. Luckily for you, **this book lets you shortcut all that and get right to the summit of spiritual enlightenment,** like a cheat code in a video game. It's pretty much the spiritual equivalent of the Konami code (Up, Up, Down, Down, Left, Right, Left, Right, B, A, Start). *Beep, boop, beep, boop.* You're holy, and you have infinite lives and all weapons unlocked as well!

While we've focused a lot of our attention so far on *looking* spiritual, now we're going to help you *actually* become spiritual in your personal life by doing all the right Christian-looking things and learning all the right Christian-sounding phrases. We'll also look at some of the major sins to avoid, especially some of the really terrible ones that cannot be forgiven, like voting for a Democrat.

The great Puritan John Owen famously wrote, "Be killing sin or it will be killing you." You must make it your aim to sanctify yourself every day of your life, beginning when you wake up each morning.

Hopefully you grew up in a Christian home and attended Awana programs as a child. Earning a few Sparks badges or even the revered Timothy Award can give you a huge leg up on the competition. A document recovered with the Dead Sea Scrolls even confirmed that presenting any completed Awana book at the gates of heaven will get you right into the fast-pass lane, bypassing the long line entirely. While those suckers without a decked-out Cubbies uniform are waiting eons to get to the front of the queue, you'll already be sipping a virgin piña colada and rubbing shoulders with Billy Graham and Chucky Spurgeon.

If you didn't do any of the required Awana work as a young lass or lad, you're definitely at a disadvantage. Still, with hard work, you can make up for your inability to recite the Awana pledge from memory.

With a little luck and a lot of hard work, even you can please the Father. So let's get started.

For those who want to be sanctified, we recommend starting each day off right by **setting your alarm clock to your local Christian radio station.** You need the latest repetitive Christian pop song or advertisement to rouse you from your slumber.

Conformity to Christian culture starts the moment you wake up each day.

You can't just stop there, however. You've got to make sure you only ever listen to Christian music **at all times.** Set *all* of your radio presets to Christian radio stations, even if all your radio picks up is that weird cult station founded by the guy who predicted the end of the world a bunch of times. If you're driving to work and you happen to hear a stray secular tune wafting into your car, roll up your windows immediately and begin screaming Philippians 4:13 at the top of your lungs to help you overcome the temptation to tap your foot to the beat of sinful music peddled by satanic artists like Taylor Swift and Journey.*

Maintain the integrity of your Christian bubble at all times. Even a small leak can lead to depressurization and spiritual compromise. Contemporary Christian music is one of the means of

---

* We know a holy person like you hasn't heard of either of these acts. But rest assured, listen to so much as a chorus from either one of them, and you're as good as damned. Not even once!

grace prescribed by the New Testament. God designed the Christian life so that cookie-cutter peppy Christian music is the crucible in which your hard-earned righteousness is painstakingly forged day by day.

But you've also got to make sure that any so-called Christians who *do* listen to secular music know how much you disdain any tunes that aren't played on your local Christian station.

Sample Conversation

CARNAL "CHRISTIAN": Hey, bro, do you remember that old Metallica album that came out when we were in high school? Good times, man.

YOU: What is a Metallica? Is that some kind of sports team? Is it on the periodic table?

CARNAL "CHRISTIAN": Uh, what? They're a massively famous heavy metal band. Surely you've heard of them?

YOU: Sorry. If they're not played on Christian radio or streaming services, I definitely haven't heard of them. In fact, I'm a little disappointed in *you* for listening to a godless band full of heathens. Would you mind standing a little farther away from me, just in case God strikes you down with a lightning bolt where you stand, O great deceiver?

This example illustrates a gravely important facet of the perfect Christian life: **always make sure to intentionally conflate your own personal convictions with biblical commands.** Whatever is unwise for you personally *must by necessity* be sinful for everyone else too. Send other Christians on a much-needed guilt trip whenever possible by continually reminding them how good you are at living up to your own man-made standards of righteousness and how much of a failure they are at doing the same.

This is also very effective when it comes to other matters of conscience, such as movies.

If you're a real Christian, then **every movie you watch ought to be a painfully bad religious film** starring a washed-up actor who couldn't get work in non-Christian movies, preferably one with a plot about the Rapture and designed to scare the life out of unbelievers. It doesn't matter how terrible the film is compared with decent secular films. It doesn't matter if it physically hurts you to observe the wooden acting and shockingly bad writing. It doesn't even matter how much it distorts the gospel. Watching Christian films is one of the best ways to sanctify your mind, *maybe* even more so than reading the Bible or praying.

You might think that watching Christian movies is too difficult, but God's Word is ready for us with words of comfort. In 2 Corinthians 4:17 (ESV), Paul tells his readers that "this light momentary affliction is preparing for us an eternal weight of glory beyond all comparison." New Testament scholars believe the "light momentary affliction" Paul was referencing was actually a low-budget Christian movie making the rounds in the ancient world. What an amazing promise that verse is, then, for the believer enduring a cringe-worthy Christian film! Every stilted line of dialogue, every two-dimensional character, and every tacked-on altar call was forged in eternity past for your sanctification. God will never give you more Christian movies than you can handle. Praise the Lord!

By way of contrast, remember that **secular movies are always sinful**. Even if a Hollywood film challenges or strengthens your faith or opens up conversations between you and nonbelievers, it is to be condemned as demon spawn from the fires of hell if it doesn't feature a sneak-attack altar call at the end.

Another great way to pull yourself up by your sanctification bootstraps is to **read lots of popular Christian books**. Amish romance novels are particularly good for your soul, as are other holy genres such as Rapture fiction and motivational self-help books. You can even double down on your sanctification by posting pictures of yourself reading said Christian books along with your massive study Bible and coffee. *Winning!*

Another storied genre of literature that is particularly helpful to the state of your soul is the **Christian adult coloring**

book. While some may think the Christian coloring book is a recent fad destined to pass into the annals of irrelevance within a few short years, archaeological discoveries peg their creation in the mid–first century, with the very first believers in Christ using them daily. The earliest extant Greek copies of the New Testament even had crude drawings of flowers, hummingbirds, and VW buses with peace-sign murals sprawled all the way across the parchment—and obscuring the text.

It's pretty clear that coloring equals holiness.

In fact, we're so certain that scribbling with crayons like a second grader is going to help you grow into a mature Christian that we've included a free Christian coloring page right here on page 115 for you to doodle. You're welcome!

Whether you're watching Christian movies in which the world lights up like a big ball of fire and only Kirk Cameron is left standing or you're reading a bonnet ripper about Jebediah the Amish farmer casting his steely gaze at Abigail the spinster, remember to turn your mind off and let your own efforts rack up credit in heaven with the Lord. Don't think critically about any of these things. They have been approved by cultural Christianity, so they're undoubtedly wholesome.

A good Christian like you needs to do more, however. You've got to go above and beyond Christian culture's call of duty. **You've got to go to the Holy Land.**

Go to Israel on a guided tour of the Bible lands, and your

perfection will be nigh. Learn all kinds of interesting facts about the Bible to put it in its proper context when you read it. Take advantage of the time to enrich your relationship with God and really dig into His Word. But most important, constantly post pictures of your trip to ensure all your friends know you're in Israel.

Your trip to Israel will continue to pay spiritual dividends long after you've returned to join the mere mortals who haven't been to the Holy Land. You can now lightly season every conversation with another Christian with phrases like "When I was standing in the very spot at which Jesus was baptized in the Jordan River . . ." and "This really reminds me of that time I stood gazing into Christ's empty tomb. You haven't done that, have you? I didn't think so." People will be so impressed with your holiness, they might just stop talking to you because they aren't worthy of your presence.

And God, too, is really, really impressed with you right about now.

Unless, of course, you have the slightest **sin** in your life. Then He's probably holding you over the pit like a spider because He loathes you so much.

Look, we don't like talking about sin. Jesus never did, and we want to follow in His footsteps. We're "red-letter Christians" in that way. Really, we've been avoiding this as long as possible.

Color this page and you will be granted fifty extra holiness points immediately credited to your spiritual bank account. Post about it on social media with the hashtag #BlessedByTheBee, and we'll double your credit! Amazing!

But once in a while, we have to get real. We need to talk about the elephant in the room: God doesn't approve of certain, seemingly innocuous activities. So for just a few minutes here, we feel compelled to address some of the biggest sins of modern Christians in order for you to remain unstained from the world. Don't worry, we'll keep it brief, and then it'll be back to constant encouragement and affirmation of your beautiful self.

Repulsive Sins Against the Lord

- **Smoking.** Jesus mentioned there was only one unforgivable sin, and it was smoking. Take so much as a half puff on a tobacco pipe, and your *eternity* is going to be the only thing that's smoking. Never smoke anything. Don't even get too close to campfires or grills.

- **Drinking.** Craft beer, wine, mixed drinks—these are all words that would fall under the umbrella of sins leading to death the apostle wrote about in 1 John 5:16–17. We know Jesus turned water into wine and never directly condemned drinking, but the truly spiritual will be able to read between the lines of the Scriptures and find the modern American aversion to alcohol. It's all there in the text if you try hard and believe in yourself.

- **Being friends with a Democrat.** Satan is the ruler of the Democratic Party and every single registered Democrat is an antichrist, so it goes without saying that you can't even know one. Unfriend them all on Facebook immediately. Cut them off from your life. And if you ever encounter one in real life, just scowl and hiss at them or punch them square in the jaw.

- **Playing Dungeons & Dragons.** A recent poll found that 81 percent of hell's inhabitants played D&D at least once a week before they were cast into the lake of fire. This shouldn't be a shock. Just look at the name—Dungeons & Dragons—and you can tell that this is satanic to the core. One D&D group in Massachusetts accidentally summoned Abaddon the Destroyer into our plane of reality when a player cast the magic missile spell incorrectly. Oops! Yeah, stay away from this one if you want any shot at making it into heaven.

- **Dancing.** You may think you're only tapping your foot to a catchy Bruno Mars song, but what you're really doing is knocking on hell's front door. Many Christians have lost their salvation by gyrating their way into the kingdom of darkness.

- **Playing cards on Sunday.** If you get invited to fill in for your cousin's sick bridge partner on a Lord's

Day, punch the demons right out of that deceiver. In fact, just to be safe, you should probably shun card playing and gambling on any day.

- **Having fun.** This is a catchall category for anything we didn't specifically name above. **The slightest moment of pleasure on this earth will echo throughout eternity as you burn in hell.** Maintain a look of somber, disciplined holiness, and the Puritans themselves will welcome you through the pearly gates.

Pull these planks out of your eye immediately, lest God decide you're not the guy or gal He wants on His team. Then, loudly and constantly call out others on the even bigger planks in their eyes. This is important.

Now for some good news: aside from the above-listed abominations, God's pretty chill about everything else.

Blech! Talking about these horrible sins makes us feel dirty. We're gonna have to throw some words of affirmation out there to cleanse the palate. Victory! Dreams! Happiness! Favor! Blessed! Champion! Ronald Reagan! College football! Barbecue ribs!

There. Much better.

Feeling perfect? Well, you shouldn't be. You're not there yet. Stop being so prideful! But, hey, you're getting close! Let's check in and see how you're doing.

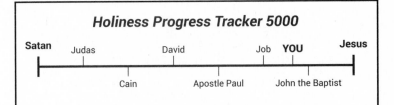

Holiness Progress Tracker 5000

Satan   Judas   David   Job   **YOU**   Jesus

Cain   Apostle Paul   John the Baptist

Hold the phone! There's only one guy left between you and Jesus. You leapfrogged right over Job himself!

You're almost there!

Keep on listening to you-centered contemporary Christian music, watching movies about the Rapture, voting Republican, and avoiding drugs, alcohol, board games, Democrats, and all forms of fun, and you'll be chillin' with Jesus in no time.

CONFORMING TO MAINSTREAM CHRISTIAN BELIEFS

Doctrine? Is that some kind of Pokémon?

—Joel Osteen

f you've followed along so far—and we know you have—then you understand the proper progression of true religion. First, you work on appearing outwardly holy with the help of your exciting, event-fueled church and your impeccable online profile. Then, you become actually holy in your personal life by following a nearly infinite list of man-made dos and don'ts dictated by culture, far above and beyond what the Scriptures teach, as you grasp toward Christian perfection.

Are you still with us?

Good.

Then the next step is to work on learning the **basic teachings of the Christian faith.**

As you can imagine, this is important stuff. So please pay attention.

Sanctification: A Biblical Progression

Righteous Appearance

⇩

Holy Living

⇩

Good Doctrine

So how do you determine what good doctrine is? With so many competing belief systems out there that fly the banner of Christ, how can you know what's true and what's false? There are actually four million books at your local Christian bookstore—the ones that are still in business anyway—so how on earth can you know which books are beacons of truth and which are destined for the fires of Gehenna?

The measuring stick the Lord left the church by which we might discern truth from error is the current beliefs of Christian culture. Whatever is in vogue in your theological camp is definitely true, but whatever teachings go against the mainstream are patently false. Coincidentally, truth often makes us feel good about ourselves while error often makes us feel bad about ourselves. **You can trust your feelings in tandem with the ever-shifting cultural standards of theological truth.**

Just go with the flow. Trust the zeitgeist. When has the modern church ever been wrong about anything?

With so many voices out there, however, it can be tough to hear the voice of truth among the deceivers who would lead you astray from popular, feel-good doctrine. We want you to be *perfect,* so we've compiled a brief systematic theology within these pages to help you know what to believe.*

THE SCRIPTURES

The Bible is the inerrant, inspired Word of God, embodied in the original Authorized King James Version of 1611, truth in all its parts, without any mixture of error. This encompasses not only the majestic Elizabethan English of the original text but also the study notes included in the Scofield Reference Bible, the Ryrie Study Bible, and the MacArthur Study Bible, respectively.

When we say the Bible is inerrant, what we mean is that it's without any error in any truth claim that it makes, **unless it contradicts any preconceived cultural or emotional viewpoints you bring to the text**. This important hermeneutical principle is called **eisegesis**. You must bring your own belief system to the Bible and contort, stretch, and butcher the text until it fits neatly in your theological box. Never let the Scriptures challenge your way of thinking.

---

* Feel free to use this as your church's statement of faith. That Baptist Faith and Message and the Westminster Confession were getting pretty long in the tooth anyway.

Speaking of the Scriptures, let's take a look at a few of the most popular translations before moving on to some important theological terms.

Bible Translations: A Handy Guide

- **ESV.** This sacred abbreviation may as well stand for "extremely spiritual version," because Christians with an ESV really care about theological truth. Pair your leather-bound, tribal-design-covered ESV with a steamy mug of black coffee for a superlegit Instagram pic.
- **NASB.** Carrying a God-fearing New American Standard Bible signals to those around you that you're not to be trifled with. Pack an eight-pound NASB and everyone will know you're a serious theologian who can shut down any theological argument at a moment's notice.
- **NIV.** If you don't want to rock the boat too much, ride the fence with the trusty, dusty New International Version. No one will be able to get a good read on your theology just from your Bible translation, so you can remain intriguing, aloof, and mysterious.
- **The Message.** When your doctrine is as soft as butter in the sunshine, you can't go wrong with this classic paraphrase of the Scriptures. It's not as much a translation as it is a compilation of random meta-

phors off the top of Eugene Peterson's head, so you know you'll never be challenged or stretched by God's actual words. Perfect!

- **Original Greek and Hebrew.** When no English translation could possibly be good enough for you, just tote around a few Byzantine text reproductions (which were translated from the King James), and you'll be sure to turn a few heads.
- **King James Version.** Before 1611, no one had any idea what the Bible said. Then the good ol' Authorized Version was sent down from on high, and the Word of God was with us in all its *thee* and *thou* perfection. Best paired with lots of incoherent screaming about every other translation's diabolic origin.

As you can see, there are big differences between the translations. The best way to navigate their differences is to get a copy of every English version, and then, when you're in a position where you need to look up a verse, flip through each one until you get the one that most represents what you want it to say. If you're tech-savvy, you can even download the Bible-Gateway app to a phone or tablet and then look up any verse in fifty-seven English translations, accepting only the rendering that makes you feel the most comfortable.

Got it? Good. Now on to some essential Christian truths you need to have under your belt.

GOD

There is only one God, who is the Creator and Ruler of the universe, infinitely holy and majestic, eternally existent in the Trinity: Father, Son, and Holy Spirit. We know that's hard to wrap your head around, so let's look at each of the Persons of the Trinity in detail.

God the Father

The Old Testament is where we learn about God the Father. He is an angry, brooding, bearded old man who sits on a cloud somewhere throwing lightning bolts and hurricanes at liberals and homosexuals. He votes Republican, loves football, and is suspicious of non-Americans and people with brown skin. He's especially proud of His finest creation—the United States of America—and is a true American patriot. He sometimes gives us new revelations through *The 700 Club*.

God the Son

While the Father is a little uptight, Jesus is really laid back. He was just a superchill communist hippie who wandered the countryside two thousand years ago and affirmed people in their sin. He would never judge you or hold you to any kind of moral standard. He is your Savior, but most important, He is your *Homeboy*. He also agrees with all of your opinions and would never challenge your beliefs or make you feel uncomfortable or convicted. Even today, Jesus is constantly adjusting and fine-tuning His character, attributes, and attitudes to perfectly line up with current thought. Jesus is just like you. Isn't that incredible?

God the Holy Spirit

In the classic theological treatise *Star Wars: A New Hope,* the great theologian Obi-Wan Kenobi tells young Luke Skywalker all about the Force. He says, "It's an energy field created by all living things. It surrounds us and penetrates us; it binds the galaxy together." Similarly, in the revered latter-day revelation called *Star Wars: The Force Awakens,* Maz Kanata tells Rey, "Close your eyes. Feel it. The light—it's always been there. It will guide you." The descriptions of the Force* from Star Wars are pretty close to what the Holy Spirit is like—maybe even more accurate than what the Bible says about Him.

He's an impersonal force whose main purpose is to make you feel really good during powerful times of worship. Whenever you feel the warm fuzzies, that's the Holy Spirit. He must be coaxed into the room like a hard-to-catch legendary Poké-mon. We recommend laser lights, fog machines, and impeccable

---

* While the Star Wars prequels suggested that the Force was simply controlled by microorganisms known as midi-chlorians, these unholy works were condemned as heresy at the Council of Nicaea in AD 325, and the members emphatically declared, "That's not how the Force works!"

stage lighting to create your best chance of getting the Spirit to move.

Above all, the Holy Spirit will never make you feel bad about sin or call you to do something you don't want to do. He will only ever cause burning feelings of great emotion in your chest in order to inspire you to do something that you already wanted to do anyway. He's pretty cool like that!

MAN

Man was created in the image of God but quickly went against the Lord's original design by dancing, playing poker and bridge, and generally making merriment. Every human being has innate value in God's eyes, except for scary immigrants, Muslims, liberals, and anyone else who makes you feel slightly uncomfortable or otherwise challenges your American cultural Christian worldview. God desires that all men be saved, but we should still preach the gospel sparingly in case He actually saves that person you really don't want to spend eternity with.

SALVATION

Jesus died on the cross for our sins, rose again on the third day, and now reigns at the right hand of the Father. You'd think this would mean believers can just rest in the Father's grace now, but you'd be wrong. You wouldn't be reading a book called *How to Be a Perfect Christian* if that were true, now would you? No, those who wish to be saved must strive, day in and day out, to appear perfectly holy and sinless. And God could take away your salvation at literally any moment, especially if He spots you in the vicinity of a bar or a restaurant other than Chick-fil-A.

Key Evidences of Salvation

- impeccably dressed on Sunday morning
- thirty years of perfect church attendance
- collected works of C. S. Lewis
- Christian fish emblem on car
- ability to find any book of the Bible in 3.2 seconds without consulting the table of contents
- proof of visiting the Holy Land at least once

THE CHURCH

We already covered this, but just to refresh your memory, the church is the visible, gathered assembly of the saints, most of whom are really annoying and none of whom understand the Bible as well as you do. The church exists to meet your needs and inflate your sense of self-importance as well as throw fun events like potlucks and movie nights. There's also a universal church, which is similar to the local church but doesn't have as many potlucks.

LAST THINGS

God will bring all things to an end, preceded by the pretribulation Rapture of the church into glory and the establishment of His visible kingdom on Earth in fulfillment of His promises to America and the church. This will all happen by 1988, according to prophecy experts who have studied blood moons and numbers and stuff. For more on biblical eschatology, we recommend watching the excellent documentary *Left Behind,* starring Kirk Cameron,* or the equally accurate *A Thief in the Night.*

Signs of the End Times

- Ozzy rejoining Black Sabbath
- the end of the Mayan calendar system
- Y2K
- blood moons, full moons, moonwalking, Russians landing on the moon, Blue Moon Belgian White beer

---

* In our opinion, the Nicolas Cage remake is trash.

- a throbbing in John Hagee's left big toe
- the release of *Half-Life 3*

Study these glorious truths as the sound doctrine they are. Marinate in them for hours, like a juicy T-bone steak. Forge your mind anew in the fires of Christian cultural beliefs.

Unfortunately, there's one caveat: **if Christian culture shifts its beliefs, you have to be ready to immediately accept any new doctrine that hits the mainstream**. You must live your life with a constant awareness that objective truth might change tomorrow, should the powers that be so decide.

If our culture decides your beliefs are offensive and archaic tomorrow, immediately drop them and declare that anyone who still holds to the belief system you held to just twenty-four hours ago is an intolerant bigot. Holding to sound doctrine is closely related to being ready to abandon your sincerely held faith the second you sense the tides of culture begin to shift against it. This is the very backbone of the Christian faith.*

Now, despite the ever-changing moral values you need to be up to speed on every moment of every day, there is still the beauty of the **unchanging gospel**.

Thus there are some essential, eternal truths of the faith,

---

* This is what Paul was talking about in 1 Corinthians 9.

dear friend, that must *never* be altered, no matter what *anyone* says. You cannot compromise on these core tenets of the faith.

Ready to learn what they are?

The Seven Essential Truths of the Gospel

1. **You are amazing.** You are so special and amazing, you've surpassed even God's expectations for your life. As the great theologian Christina Aguilera said, "You are beautiful. . . . Words can't bring you down!"

2. **God really needs you on His team.** What would God do without you? God decided to save sinners because He was really lonely and needed you to cheer Him up.

3. **God is love and has absolutely no other distinguishing attributes.** Holiness? Justice? Wrath? Sovereignty? Nah. God is *love* and only love.

4. **Jesus died for your temporary comfort and security.** You were just so special that God sent His only Son so you could be satisfied with temporary things of this earth.

5. **Did we mention you're amazing?** Seriously, we just can't even describe how amazing you are. Turn

your eyes upon yourself, and the things of earth
will grow strangely dim.

6. **The God of the Bible would never do anything you
would personally disagree with.** God is constantly
checking His actions against your subjective moral
compass to make sure you're never offended. He's
lucky you're around to keep Him on message!

7. **Those who conform to cultural Christianity will be
justified.** You will be declared right with God only
when you look like a really good Christian. It's a
hard road, but it'll be worth it in the end. We
promise!

Isn't that beautiful?

You must preach this gospel of your own sufficiency to save
yourself each and every day if you want to remain focused on
your sacred mission to become a perfect Christian. Listen to
preachers who do nothing but encourage you, lift you up, and
constantly remind you just how worthy you are of God's grace.
Avoid any kind of negativity, including any books or sermons
that would dare suggest you are a great sinner in need of a great
Savior.

With any luck, your mind is now renewed by the power of
your own imagination and will, all reinforced by the glorious
truths of the Christian faith we have laid out in this chapter.

Let's see if the Holiness Tracker agrees.

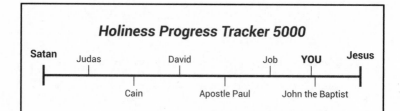

You made more progress, but you didn't quite pass John the Baptist. Not surprising because he was superholy, with all of his eating locusts and living in the wilderness and baptizing Jesus and whatnot.

You're going to have to kick it into high gear to pass ol' JTB. Get going, you're almost there!

Eight

QUARANTINING YOUR HOME FROM THE WORLDLY WASTELANDS

A locked and barricaded home is part of Christian responsibility and should be practiced to the level of capacity.

—Francis Schaeffer

t's been said that a man's home is his castle, his refuge from the pressures and stresses of the world. But for the perfect Christian, your home isn't a castle, **your home is a mighty fortress,** one outfitted with massive laser turrets, thirty-foot-thick concrete walls, a panic bunker, and a one-hundred-yard-wide moat to keep out the dangers of the outside world. Your home should be the spiritual equivalent of the Death Star,* but without a fatal flaw in the form of an exhaust port just large enough for a pair of proton torpedoes to slip in and blow up the whole thing.

See, if you want to protect your family from ever sinning, and you desire to see them join you on your lofty perch

---

* This is another Star Wars reference, if you didn't catch it.

of perfection, **you need to learn how to quarantine your home from the wily wastelands of the world.** You need to discover the important disciplines of meeting the right mate, conforming the hierarchy of your home to culturally Christian standards, keeping everyone else out, and raising your children to never, ever make a mistake—just like you.

Think about how much better the world would be if you raised an entire family of your very own clones, each just as amazing as you are.

It's time to begin exploiting your family for the advancement of your glory. Whether you're single, dating, er, excuse us, courting, or married, your relationships are stepping-stones on the journey to perfection.

But the good Christian begins laying the seeds for a mighty fortress of a home years before they're married and forbidding their children to participate in Halloween.* It all starts with **attending youth group as an adolescent.**

The main reason to go to church when you're a young whippersnapper is to begin a personal relationship with the cute boy or girl in the youth worship band. Sure, the free pizza and wacky youth games are fun, but don't lose focus: you're here to get a mate! Don't worry about looking for godly qualities like character or integrity. It's all about how hot your potential mate looks while singing Hillsong tunes onstage. If your

---

* Obviously Halloween is out of the question.

special someone is seen as a good Christian by others, then, by association, they'll begin to see you the same way.

Make sure your potential mate wears something modest, such as floor-length denim dresses if you really want to adhere to tradition (in the case of a girl) or polo shirts tucked into their Sunday slacks (in the case of a guy). You really want to go for an Amish look. When a boy and a girl lock eyes during the chorus of "In the Secret," you know that it was destined to be since before the foundation of the world. So plop on down next to that fine catch on the next youth group bus trip to Disneyland or the nearest knockoff theme park and ask if they want to go steady.

When things do get serious, you need to make sure you avoid using the d-word: dating. You and your partner should kiss dating goodbye like good Christians and immediately begin a holy courtship, as the Bible teaches.

Courting is like dating, but for righteous people. Go visit the home of that one family at your church that has twenty-eight kids and observe the beauty of the godly courting relationships that their youngsters foster with other families as large and holy as they are. To be honest, we're not sure what the difference is between dating and courting, but we know that God loves those who court, while dating is one of the six or seven things He hates. It's in the Bible somewhere, we think.

Starting a holy courtship when you're twelve years old is just the beginning.

When you turn eighteen and go to a local unaccredited Bible college like a good Christian, your singular mission should be to find a mate within three days of arriving and get married before the first school year is up (get that "ring by spring," ladies!). We recommend carrying around a twenty-page checklist of everything you require in a mate in order for them to meet your lofty standards, and then loudly questioning every member of the opposite sex that walks by to see if they are up to code.

We've included a few ideas to get you started.

Preliminary Checklist for the Ideal Mate

- owns entire DC Talk discography
- totes well-worn copy of *I Kissed Dating Goodbye* at all times
- wears denim skirt or khaki pants
- has WWJD bracelet securely and unironically fastened around wrist, ankle, and so on
- owns T-shirt with Christian slogan, preferably a parody of a secular brand
- carries Scofield Reference Bible with highlighting throughout
- has been on at least fifteen short-term mission trips

Don't worry about working on your own imperfections and sins; concentrate on getting the numerous repulsive specks out of your future husband or wife's eye, as Jesus talked about. Once you've found "the one," get married as soon as possible. God can't accomplish His will in your life if you're single! Like, why are you not married yet? We're waiting . . .

Once you're finally married by age twenty-one like the godly man or woman you are, you'll be forced to choose between two ways you can run your home: hardcore, red-blooded complementarianism or radical, tree-hugging egalitarianism. So let's take a look at these two methods of running your home. **Study each carefully, pray about your decision for at least five seconds, and then select the system you'll wholeheartedly adopt as sacred Scripture between the four walls of your home.**

THE SACRED TEACHINGS
OF COMPLEMENTARIANISM

Complementarian Men

These men must rule their home as ruthlessly as supreme leader Kim Jong-un runs the great Democratic People's Republic of Korea. Every minute household decision must be run by the husband, and he gets the final say—no ifs, ands, or buts about it. In Ephesians 5, Paul addresses how men are to run their homes, and he's pretty clear that the Lord calls men to be unilateral, totalitarian dictators, like Big Brother or the Dark Lord Sauron.

You can put this into practice right away. Let's say your wife wants to settle in and watch a lame show on TV. She pops a bag of popcorn, curls up on the couch, and starts flipping through the Netflix catalog to find her favorite snooze fest series. This is a perfect time to exercise your biblical mandate to dominate. A four-season *Fixer Upper* marathon might fly in those namby-pamby egalitarian homes, but not on your watch. You're a biblical complementarian!

Simply furrow your brow, shake your head, and flash a thumbs-down like that guy in *Gladiator*. Then say something like, "Honey, I love you, and because I long for your sanctification, we're not going to be watching this show about remodeling homes and using ridiculous amounts of shiplap tonight. Instead, we'll be watching *SportsCenter*. You will be expected to take notes." Then enthrone yourself on your La-Z-Boy recliner and signal for your lady to fetch you a grape soda.

The ideal complementarian male will never take his wife's opinion into account. You must rule with an iron fist. Every mundane decision is part and parcel of your spiritual directive to make sure your wife knows who is in charge.

Complementarian Women

Your job is to make sure every whim of your husband's is fulfilled. Your job is to be his helpmeet (which roughly translates from the original Greek to "happy slave"). While he watches *SportsCenter,* you get the joy and honor of bringing him buffalo wings and soda. Don't make the mistake of ever challenging him on any decisions, even if it might seem like a small thing, such as what you're going to have for dinner or what color the throw pillows should be. God *is* in the center of every decision, big or small, and you must let your husband make the final call without question.

When your husband mercifully allows you to go outdoors to buy groceries, be sure to always walk a half step behind him. Keep your eyes cast downward. Only speak when spoken to. You exist solely as an extension of your husband, so be sure to keep him happy at all times.

THE BLESSED DOCTRINES OF EGALITARIANISM

Now, we aren't going to mince words with you. **Egalitarianism is far less holy than tried-and-true complementarianism.** But we'll have grace on you if that's how you feel the Lord is calling you to run your little home.

See how gracious we are? One day you'll be as merciful and loving as we.

Egalitarian Men

In an egalitarian household, your wife has the right to do whatever she wants, whenever she wants, regardless of consequences. Never challenge her on anything. If she decides to stop going to church, say nothing. If she is struggling with a sin and could really use some support, just back off and give her space to be her own person. If she decides to leave you in order to join a cult that's planning on launching a starship to seek out the colonies of the legendary planet Kobol in the dim reaches of space, you need to affirm her in her decision. It is the twenty-first century, after all, not the Dark Ages.

Your wife is an independent woman, therefore you should never do anything that could be construed as taking the lead. We recommend that egalitarian husbands are never to be the breadwinners. In fact, you probably shouldn't contribute financially to the family at all. Instead, you should play the latest *Madden NFL* game on your Xbox all day long and rest in the knowledge that you're not being a burden on the home. You are, instead, *empowering* your wife to work eighty-hour weeks to pay your family's mortgage. There's no better way to be a godly husband. And you don't want to be oppressive and lead your home like those backward complementarians, do you?

Egalitarian Women

Your job is to violently oppose any traditional gender or marriage norms at all costs, regardless of your personal interests. This is called "smashing the patriarchy." If your husband says something seemingly harmless like, "Hey, what should we have for dinner?" it's time to blast him. "What do you mean, *'What should we have for dinner?'* Do I look like your personal chef?! Isn't this the twenty-first century?! Make yourself dinner, you sexist Puritan!" Should you so much as make a sandwich for your husband, even on a special occasion like his birthday, you'll undo all the advancements feminism has brought you over the past century, and you'll become a traitor to your sex.

To further ensure the advancement of women, you must always prioritize your career over any desire you may have to start a family. However, should you do decide to have kids, be sure to still aggressively work full time while using the remaining hours in the day to be a present, involved, and nurturing mother. You can have it all, which is what the good Lord intended.

Now, you might think you can just run your home according to the Bible without vocally committing to one of these marital frameworks, but that's not an option for the perfect Christian. You must cast your lot with the extremes of one of these two camps, and then judge any married couples who don't measure up to your rigid system. Your man-made framework for marriage might as well be Scripture.*

Of course, everyone knows **the purpose of a biblical marriage is to produce truckloads of cherubic children. We**

---

* In fact, go ahead and scribble in your man-made ideas about home and marriage in those blank pages in the back of your Bible. Now your opinions are as good as Scripture. Neat!

recommend having at least eighteen kids to advance the kingdom of God. Look down with derision on any couples who choose not to have kids or to only have three or four. They're clearly selfish heathens at heart.

When you do have kids, it's imperative that you **begin the quarantining process early.** While the child is in the womb, play lots of John Piper and John MacArthur sermons at high volume for the developing baby. When he finally enters the world, name him something like Calvin, Graham, Spurgeon, or even Jesus. Girl babies are best named something like Hannah, Ruth, Abigail, or Piper. The name should reflect your all-consuming passion for letting people know how much you love theology. And don't bother with reading your kid mind-numbing tripe like Dr. Seuss's *One Fish, Two Fish, Red Fish, Blue Fish.* Start with Calvin's *Institutes* for the first few weeks of your infant's life, and then graduate to some Machen or N. T. Wright before their first birthday.*

We recommend not allowing your kids to have any contact with any remotely non-Christian influences for at least the first twenty-five years of their lives. The only movies they are allowed to watch should be Psalty the Singing Song Book sing-alongs, *The Chronicles of Narnia* films (the old BBC versions, not the evil Disney interpretations), and *VeggieTales* (nothing after the *Jonah* movie, when the liberals took the franchise

---

* Don't forget the matchless power of the Internet: staging a picture of your three-day-old "reading" Luther's *On the Bondage of the Will* is worth tons of Jesus points.

over). Never let them learn to appreciate films as art. Rather, movies should be used exclusively as vehicles for modifying your children's behavior, even if their hearts are still totally unregenerate.

When it comes to music, they should learn the "Books of the Bible Song" and "Father Abraham" obviously, but **never let them listen to any secular songs,** no matter how innocent they may appear at first glance. One minute, they're innocently humming along with Hanson's *MMMBop,* and the next, they're uttering Satanic spells that summon Beelzebub the Deceiver in dark, unholy rituals with their neighborhood coven.

The smallest crack in the armor of your Christian home could lead to ruin.

As in your conversations with other Christians, turn absolutely everything into a teaching moment. When your kid is superexcited for finally getting his first hit in a Little League game, don't just offer him congratulations, a juice box, and some orange slices. Instead, remind him that his grounder that skipped past the shortstop was preordained by God before the foundations of the world. When he sprains his ankle and screams in pain, remind him that what he is feeling is nothing compared to the pain Christ went through on the cross. Don't allow any moment to get by without showing your kids—and other parents—how sanctified your renewed mind is.

This brings us to the question of education. You could send your kids to public school, but only if you hate them and want them to turn into empty-headed, liberal, atheist, fascist drones. Or you could send them to a local Christian school. This is obviously a better choice, but it's still not the best.

Perfect Christians know that **true believers homeschool.** Of all the millions of things you can say to impress a fellow Christian, nothing holds a candle to the wide-eyed looks of awed admiration you will receive when you utter these four holy words: "I homeschool my kids."

Now when it comes to the homeschooling curriculum, it should consist primarily of end-times Rapture charts and visits to creation museums. If you're not visiting a creation museum with your kids and showing them lifelike dioramas of Jesus riding dinosaurs with Adam and Eve in the garden approximately six thousand years ago, then you might as well be sending them to the godless public-school government indoctrination camp down the street. Skip so much as one trip to the museum, and the next thing you know your kids will be getting face tattoos, piercing their noses, doing meth, and sneaking out to Taylor Swift concerts.

But giving your kids a good education isn't enough. **Make sure to work the fact that you homeschool into every conversation.** You don't get any spiritual credit for teaching your second grader scientific ideas like young-earth creationism and dispensational, pretribulation premillennialism if you don't constantly mention the fact that you homeschool to every passerby you encounter. Make sure any mom who chooses to send her kids to public school knows just how much of a spiritual loser she is.

Homeschooling is not just your personal conviction, it's a biblical mandate!

Coupled with your knowledge of using the Internet to increase your fame and widen your spheres of influence, the experience of raising kids can even be leveraged into a lucrative mom blog (sorry dads, women have the edge here). Pretend that you know what you're doing, fake that you have it all together, and start blogging. Start every blog post with "You guyyyyyyssss," and then make some kind of profound-sounding statement about your "beautifully messy" life by drawing a superficial connection between the Cheetos your kids spilled in the back of your forty-passenger van that morning to the persecution of Christians that our Savior warned about in the gospels. You'll have hundreds of thousands of Christian women following your advice in no time.

It's a brutal world out there. With proper isolation methods, your home will become a bastion of holiness for years to come. Remember, your family exists for the express purpose of zealously defending your particular expression of Christianity from any outside influences, not to share the love of Christ with your neighbors.

So raise your spiritual drawbridge and batten down the hatches!

Holiness Progress Tracker 5000

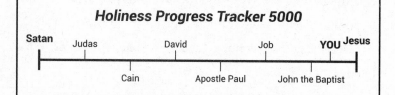

They said you'd never make it.
They said it was impossible.

But sure enough, here you are: holier
than John the Baptist and creeping
right up on Jesus Himself.

WOW!

CRUSADING AGAINST THE HEATHENS

What is best in life is to crush your theological opponents, to see them schooled by your mad logical arguments, and to hear the lamentations of the heathen.

—Conan the Cimmerian

The idols—there were thousands of them—lined the street on either side of the apostle as he slowly strolled through the city. Altars to eldritch gods, horrifying monstrosities. Statues built in service of demons, whose evil grip on the city grew day by day. The monuments to the false gods stabbed the morning sky, unholy symbols of the people's arrogant defiance of the God who had made them.

Well, the apostle Paul was downright triggered, and he wasn't gonna take it anymore.

According to the Bible, the man himself ambled right up to the mayor of Athens and leveled him with a brutal haymaker. Then he started break dancing all up on the Areopagus in celebration of his complete and total victory over the heathen gods while those watching called out, "Dang, son!" and "Got 'em, coach!" Paul followed it up with an altar call, and that day hundreds were converted to the gospel as they saw Paul's mad skills at crushing his theological foes. Then Paul put his tent-making talents to work by designing dozens of provocative picket signs and organizing a protest of all the local non-Christian businesses and government buildings.

We're not making this up. You can read the historical account in Acts 17.*

If you're going to be perfect, you have to learn how to share the gospel effectively. **And the best way to do this is to totally own your opponents, arguing them into the faith through the sheer brilliance of your intellect.** Combine this with a healthy sense of your own importance, and you'll be shepherding thousands of people into the kingdom. Lock and load, fellow Christian. Nuke the heathen from orbit. It's the only way to be sure.

Much of modern evangelism has focused on how to effectively present the gospel and bring people to an understanding of their need for a Savior. *This is wrong!* The goal in any evangelistic activity is to show off your advanced theological knowledge and to make the heathen understand that they are much less holy than you are. Forget about building relationships: a

---

* Remember, if your translation doesn't agree with our account, get a different translation.

successful evangelistic endeavor is one in which you scream "You're going to hell, sinner!" as many times as possible. Seriously, count how many times you scream that exact phrase and gauge the quality of each of your evangelistic efforts by that measuring stick.

This whole aggressive-evangelism thing can be difficult at first, because you might have been raised in a Christian tradition that taught that you should love even those who don't believe exactly the same things you do, that the best way to share the gospel is to build bridges, attempt to understand where others are coming from, and find common ground with nonbelievers.

Yuck!

Over against these unbiblical methods of evangelism, we recommend learning to harbor a healthy disdain for everyone who isn't a Christian. When you start seeing other people as less than human, it's much easier to scream vulgarities at them to the glory of God. You earned your salvation fair and square while they choose to wallow in their ignorance and not pull themselves up by their spiritual bootstraps. So it's time to begin thinking of unbelievers not as fellow image bearers desperately in need of God's grace but as vermin who threaten the very existence of your comfortable Christian subculture.

It's time to get creative. **Let's dig into some of the awesome methods of evangelism and outreach that have been used by God's people since the days of Noah.**

One great way to get the message of God's love out there is to **make offensive signs** to attract attention and let people know just how much God hates them, just as the apostle Paul did at Mars Hill. Then organize a protest at absolutely every event in the area that doesn't line up with your idea of what God likes: community picnics (tools of the New World Order), secular rock-and-roll concerts (unsanitary cesspools of sin), and even seniors square dancing night at the community center (square dancing is still dancing, after all).

Effective Evangelistic Picket Signs

God hates you

Hell = Your final destination

God chose me not you LOL

Honk if you love Jesus—Remain silent if you
      love Satan

You and all your loved ones are doomed. Have
      a great day!

Just before Christ ascended into heaven, He commissioned His disciples to go into all the world and preach the gospel by offending as many people as possible. So buy the biggest megaphone you can find, make some eye-catching, controversial signs that put people in their place, and start spreading the love of Christ. You want to start a God-centered conversation with people by making sure that only your opinions are ever heard, that they're unable to get a word in edgewise. Just be reasonable and scream all kinds of obscenities at unbelievers whenever it appears they are about to express an opinion.

If you really care about people's eternal fate, you'll need to do more than just picket soldier's funerals and comic book conventions. If you're agile, you could pull off some **advanced ambush evangelism,** first popularized by Pentecostal street preachers in the 1920s. Hide in the bushes in a crowded public place. Lie in wait, carefully looking over your potential targets. You'll want to select a victim with a tattoo, piercing, or other obvious evidence of reprobation. Then, at the opportune time, leap out with a King James Bible and just deck 'em.* They'll have plenty of time to contemplate the great mercy of God in the gospel as they recover in the local hospital's trauma ward. Great job!

Evangelism happens even when you're not audibly screaming at people. As the Bible says, "Preach the gospel at all times. If necessary, use words." To this end, you need to **deck yourself out in T-shirts plastered with clever Christian parodies of popular brands and slogans.** A recent study found that more than 97 percent of believers came to faith in Christ after spotting a believer's "A Bread Crumb & Fish" or "Lord's Gym"

---

* Bonus evangelism points if you use a Ryrie, Scofield, or MacArthur Study Bible.

T-shirt. If you're really committed, you'll burn all your non-Christian T-shirts in a bonfire this instant, run down to your local megachurch's bookstore, and replace them all with sanctified Christian culture–approved versions.

Your car, too, ought to be an extension of your evangelistic strategy. **Plaster that puppy in judgmental bumper stickers.**

*Top Ten Most Effective Christian Bumper Stickers**

In case of Rapture, this car will be unmanned

Don't let the car fool you—my treasure is in heaven!

If it ain't King James, it ain't the Bible!

God said it, I believe it, that settles it

Follow me to the creation museum

I'd rather be singing hymns

Don't be left behind

I hope you follow Jesus this closely

My boss is a Jewish carpenter

Too blessed to be stressed!

Every waking moment of your life can be devoted to evangelism. Even cutting someone off in traffic can be redeemed to

---

* Ranked by average number of people converted each year, according to a 2016 LifeWay Research poll.

the glory of God with the right combination of Christian bumper stickers. Let no square inch of your car's bumper or rear window remain untouched by clever slogans designed to shout to others on the freeway just how much you love Jesus. A well-placed TRUTH fish eating a four-legged Darwin fish can do more for the kingdom of God than many hours of street evangelism. And don't settle for the stock, reprobate license-plate frame advertising Frank's World of Cars. Get yourself a sanctified frame with Jeremiah 29:11 or Philippians 4:13 engraved on that bad boy.

So deck out your whip. Someone's eternal fate may depend on it.

You can even change the eternal fate of waiters and waitresses by **leaving a Bible verse on your credit card receipt instead of a tip.** Scribble something down like "God only gets 10%—why would you think you deserve 15%?" and follow it up with "John 3:16—Jesus Loves You!"

We'll get into gospel tracts a little later, but advanced Christian diners can even leave a tract that looks like a trillion-dollar bill so your server is fooled into thinking she's getting a good tip before she gets sucker punched with the good news. This trick works best after a three-hour lunch on a Sunday, while you and your Christian friends all wear official church T-shirts. Make sure to be overly demanding and never satisfied with anything the server does to make your meal right. Every second your waiter or waitress is forced to spend serving you is another second in which your holiness is rubbing off on them.

But no matter your preferred style of outreach, remember that **evangelism is not so much about quality as it is about quantity.**

You know how American pilots during World War II would mark their planes with how many Messerschmitts they shot down over Europe or how many Zeros they sent to a watery grave in the Pacific? You need to do the same thing with any pagans you convert to Christ. Keep a running tab of how many sinners you drag kicking and screaming into the kingdom by your own clever preaching.

You need to puff up your own ego by getting thousands of people saved, no matter how inauthentic their professions of faith may seem on the surface. You've probably already seen your pastor do this during his altar calls each week. **You might even have gone down yourself to save everyone the pain of sitting there and having to listen to the pastor beg for eons.** Each sinner who raises his hand and comes forward is a notch in the pastor's belt. Even if the gospel wasn't preached accurately. Even if there was no conviction of sin. Even if the cross wasn't mentioned a single time. If a sinner walks to the front of the church, no matter what his motive, you'd darn well better believe it counts.

See, your pastor has his priorities straight: Generate tons of baptisms and confessions of faith. Churn 'em out like a factory assembly line. Commitments to Christ are very healthy for the megachurch pastor's ego, and they can be just as good for your own if you're faithful to dilute the gospel to the point where it's palatable to almost anyone. Get that conversion. Really go for it, like those guys selling cleaning products on late-night television or that used-car salesman who promises he's gonna club a baby seal if you don't run on down to the car lot this instant and buy a preowned Chevy S-10 pickup for full MSRP.

Faithful evangelism also has the fortunate side effect of boosting your reputation among your fellow churchgoers.

Don't even bother evangelizing if you're not going to post online about it or at least tell every single Christian you know how well you presented the gospel. Begin every conversation with a brother or sister in Christ with, "Did I ever tell you about the time I made a Muslim loudly weep on an airplane through my vast knowledge of the Scriptures? Totally owned 'em." Shout the story from the rooftops until everyone is sick of it. Don't ever be discouraged. They are just jealous that you're a modern-day Billy Graham and they're just washed-up nobodies who couldn't evangelize their way out of a paper bag.

Now, some of us are shy. It's difficult for shy people to get out there and evangelize. But you're not off the hook even if you're an introvert. For people like you, the Lord invented **the gospel tract.**

Introduced for the first time by the early church fathers circa AD 100, the gospel tract quickly became one of the most effective ways to evangelize. Rather than talking to people and building relationships, Christians could now just leave fiery Chick tracts in public restrooms, bookstores, bus seats, and homeless people's change cups in lieu of money.

The ideal gospel tract has a few elements. First, it has a catchy title. Something like "Did You Know That You're Going to Hell?" or "28 Proofs the NIV Was Translated by Satan Himself" is going to hook people right off the bat. Next, a good gospel tract has really hokey illustrations, second only to the cartoons depicting Charles Darwin with a set of satanic horns adorning every page of a self-published young-earth creationist textbook. Finally, a good gospel tract ends with a high-pressure sales pitch in which the reader is called to either mail the tract to a fundamentalist organization of churches somewhere in northern Idaho or check the box marked "No, I would rather burn in hell."

On the facing page is an example of an ideal effective gospel tract. Feel free to tear the page out and leave it somewhere to save a soul!

If gospel tracts sound right up your alley, pick out some of your favorites—preferably tracts with cartoons picturing the devil and hell to scare people into the kingdom—and start spreading tens of thousands of them around your town.

This is the most important day of your life.

DO YOU WANT TO GO TO HELL?

Check one please:

☐ Yes   ☐ No

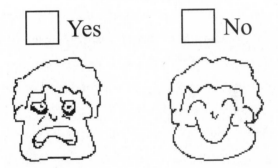

If you chose YES, then you are going to HELL!

If you chose NO, then CONGRATULATIONS, you are now a CHRISTIAN!

Please write to us and let us know of your new eternal life in Jesus Christ!

This is perhaps most efficiently done with a fully automatic gospel-tract assault rifle, which you can use to just blast people right in the face with a whole bundle of tracts before they have a chance to say, "No thanks, bud." Legendary street evangelist Ray Comfort is also reportedly developing a gospel tract–equipped Predator drone, which will be able to deliver gospel-tract payloads at Mach 1.3 all over the world from the comfort of your own home. Ah, the wonders of modern technology! It's not just for sinners anymore.

When it comes down to it, we need to recognize that we all have different evangelism personalities. Some are gifted at tearing down unbelievers one on one, some excel at picketing Comic-Con, and some are better at blasting people with gospel-tract cannons at point-blank range. Pray that the Lord would reveal how He wants you to spread the good news of how much better you are than everyone else.

No matter how the Lord has gifted you, it's your responsibility to get out there and subjugate the pagans with your awe-inspiring holiness and unparalleled theological knowledge. Jesus died for you; the least you can do is slam people of other religions for Him!

Simply and faithfully proclaiming the gospel of God's grace might have been enough in years past, but this is the twenty-first century. **It's time to get out there and kick off a hate-fueled crusade against the heathens for Jesus.**

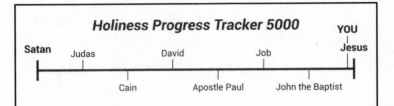

You've crested the hill and now you're breathing down Jesus's neck! You must have converted thousands to Christ since you started reading this chapter. Nice!

You're almost there! It's all downhill from here. Look at you go!

Ten

FIGHTING ON
THE FRONT LINES
OF THE CULTURE WAR

Preach the gospel at all times. If necessary, use the voting booth.

—Francis of Assisi

Most surviving gospel manuscripts state that when Jesus rode into Jerusalem in His triumphal entry, He immediately went to the temple to confront Israel's cold, dead form of Judaism. But most of these manuscripts are missing an important parenthetical narrative that was recently discovered to be part of the original text of Luke's gospel:

> And Jesus entered the voting booth and began to check all the boxes for Republican candidates. And seeing certain Jews entering the polling place and casting their votes for Democrats, he began to cry out, "I intended for my people to belong only to the GOP, but you have turned this nation into a bunch of bleeding-heart

libbies!" And He began to flip over tables like a crazy person, screaming something about making Rome great again.*

This important aside clues us in on Jesus's true intentions: to establish His kingdom through a political party, **namely, the Republicans**. The church's endgame is to institute its rule throughout the land and force the unregenerate to conform to Christian morals and beliefs. This is why God chose America as His covenant people. He knew we had what it takes to usher in an age of kingdom prosperity and holy living. Israel couldn't get the job done, so He called up the "land of the free and the home of the brave" to close the deal.

Look, you've almost made it. You've cleaned up your act, gotten yourself rid of horrible sins like watching secular movies and listening to music with a diabolical 4/4 drumbeat, and adjusted your doctrines to line up with your subjective feelings.

But conforming to church culture and becoming person-ally holy is simply not enough. If you really want to be perfect, there is still one thing you lack: **you need to join the Republican Party and to fight in the culture war.** The Christian fish decal and clever, self-righteous Christian bumper stickers on the back of your car are a good start, but you really need to add some

---

* This excerpt was taken out and covered up by the Catholic Illuminati. Read *The Da Vinci Code* for more riveting historical information.

awesome political bumper stickers that tell people how serious you are about advancing the party of Christian apostles like Ronald Reagan, Rush Limbaugh, and Bill O'Reilly. Plaster your humble ride with thousands of Far-Right slogans to signal your superiority over godless Democrats.

Joining a right-wing political party is an essential part of becoming a Christian. Trying to advance the kingdom of God through evangelism, outreach, and loving people the way Christ did can only get you so far. Those things are great, don't get us wrong, but eventually you'll need to try to elect Christian candidates to office so the power of God can *really* begin to transform culture and change lives for Jesus. Your "I Voted" sticker, according to many leading evangelical theologians, will catapult you to the VIP areas in heaven when you die.

How else would you "virtue signal" other believers that you believe in all the correct social policies that make you a perfect Christian? Christians must constantly flaunt their support for whatever social movement makes them look best in the eyes of the culture and in the eyes of their fellow brothers and sisters in Christ. Quietly living out the love of Christ in ordinary ways is so last century. Instead, you need to rock the vote for Jesus!

There are, of course, only two political parties in existence for you to join. **One of them is the enemy and the other one is God's chosen vehicle for blessing America.**

Let's take a look at each.

DEMOCRATS

You could become a tried-and-true, blue-blooded, bleeding-heart Democrat.

Spoiler alert: this is the wrong decision!

The Democratic Party was founded in 1883 as the dying wish of Karl Marx because he wanted to infiltrate this once God-fearing nation with his evil communist ideas. With the help of dark, mystical incantations and the full forces of the armies of hell, he succeeded in establishing a commie foothold in the United States, and the Democratic Party was born. Policy positions include support for gun control, abortion, big government, slightly less war than Republicans want, and slightly more assistance for the poor than Republicans are willing to offer.

Becoming a Democrat is the sin leading to death the apostle John mentioned. When Paul wrote that our struggle isn't against flesh and blood but against "the spiritual forces of evil in the heavenly places" (Ephesians 6:12, ESV), he was referencing the Democratic Party. So, from a biblical standpoint, it's really not doable to be both a Christian and a liberal. Sorry!

REPUBLICANS

If you're a good Christian, you already know what the **right** choice is. Go with the party of Abraham Lincoln, Ronald Reagan, and God: the GOP (which stands for God's Own Party).

Republicans can trace their origins all the way back to a fateful day in 1987 on which President Reagan reclined on the Oval Office sofa to watch the revered Chuck Norris film *The Delta Force* on VHS. Touched by Norris's patriotic mowing down of scores of evil Lebanese terrorists, Reagan declared the birth of a new party: the Republicans. Republican policies include support for assault rifles, prolife policies, slightly smaller government, slightly more war, and slightly less government assistance.

Republicans get to harp on all kinds of cool talking points, like accusing the "libtard" Democrats of threatening our way of life simply because they support slightly more government intervention than they do. Republicans also get to voice their support for the bombing of any country that sounds remotely Middle Eastern, even if you can't locate it on a map. **And Republicans are the chosen defenders of the sacred truth that America is God's people.**

Those liberal Democrats *hate* America and only you can save her!

Owning tons of guns as a diehard Republican is just a bonus here, but it is a sweet one. Democrats have to watch their mouths with you, because they know you're probably packing heat all the time.

There is no third political option. You have to cast your lot with one of the two establishment parties, just as the good Lord intended. And the choice is obvious. **Become a Republican or lose your salvation and suffer the eternal wrath of God.** Every moment you rightly suffer in hell, you'll be thinking, *I wish I had mailed in my Republican membership registration form like my grandma kept telling me to.*

Actually you didn't choose the Republican Party. The Republican Party chose you.

Now that you've made the correct choice and joined the GOP, you need to learn how to engage the leftists you may encounter, despite your best efforts to avoid them.

Remember to blast people on the Internet who don't agree with your political choices, as we discussed in chapter 5. Any conversation with one of the evil people on the other side of the aisle from you should be designed to show your superiority. Never honestly consider the other side's perspective. The goal of any argument ought to be to demonstrate how right you are and to blast the enemy into submission. This is how you show the love of Jesus to a dying world.

Helpful Terms for Arguing with Democrats Online

- Libtard
- Snowflake
- I'm not a racist, but . . .

- Pull yourself up by your own bootstraps
- Food-stamp junkie
- Godless commie

We also suggest familiarizing yourself with the most up-to-date meme formats you can use to mock people who disagree with you. The best way to engage in conversation with those of opposing worldviews is to misrepresent their positions using a hilarious meme or graphic, and then plaster it all over the Internet. Don't bother with ensuring the meme or graphic accurately depicts reality. The important thing is that you score imaginary Internet points in the form of likes, upvotes, retweets, or shares. If you later discover that you shared something untrue, never retract your post. *Stay strong.* The goal of crushing liberalism justifies the means of sharing inaccurate material. And be sure to tag your political opponents in these posts so they're painfully reminded of how superior your position is.

But we do have a word of warning for you, brave Christian-Republican soldier. The most important thing you can remember as you bravely head off to the front lines to fight for Jesus in the culture wars is this:

You are always being persecuted.

Got it? If your local Walmart stocks even one card that says "Happy Holidays!" or "Season's Greetings!" during the Christmas season, **you are being persecuted**. If your boss at Best Buy makes you go home to change out of your obnoxious neon-colored WWJD T-shirt, **you are being persecuted**. If the police knock on your door at 3 a.m. and ask you to turn down your Petra cassette tape that's blaring throughout the neighborhood: **You. Are. Being. Persecuted!**

The slightest offense, the most inane comment, the briefest glance of disapproval—each of these is an assault on your Christian liberties.

The handy chart on the facing page will help you identify more forms of persecution.

Should the persecution get to be too much for you to bear, consider moving to a place like China or North Korea. There is much less persecution of Christians over there, so you can immediately begin living "your best life now" with the loving support of Kim Jong-un and his pro-Christian regime. Also, Somalia's nice this time of year as well. Really, anywhere on the globe is easier to be a Christian than in the United States since the liberals began to take over God's chosen country.

But if you decide to bravely stick it out with the persecuted church in America, there is a powerful weapon you can use in fighting the culture war: **the boycott**.

The boycott was invented by famed Puritan preacher Jonathan Edwards after a waiter at his favorite New England clam chowder restaurant failed to say "God bless you" when he sneezed. Edwards organized a massive protest against the facility, and eventually it was shut down and the server was rightfully hanged for his crimes against humanity. From that moment on, the boycott was an accepted practice for Christians everywhere.

Type of Oppression	Level of Persecution
A friend invites you over to play video games but only has secular games like *Halo* or *Call of Duty* instead of sanctified titles like *Bible Adventures*.	3/10 — Persecution, but you can bear it if you believe in yourself.
A coworker offers you a secular Altoid instead of a sanctified Testamint.	5/10 — You are pressed but not crushed. Hang in there!
Another driver cuts you off on the freeway despite clearly seeing your Christian fish decal.	7/10 — Right about on the level of being burned by Nero.
Your next-door neighbor puts a sign supporting a political candidate you disagree with in their lawn.	11/10 — You are actually being persecuted more than Jesus. You must be doing something right! Now attack!

So when in doubt, boycott something. **Heck, boycott everything.** A really spiritual person has at least fifty-eight boycotts going on at any given time: Disney, Target, Starbucks, Walmart, and whatever business is unlucky enough to attract your righteous indignation. The target of the boycott doesn't matter as much as the frequency and volume with which you're able to spread the news that you're boycotting something. It's a really effective way to show how spiritually minded you are. While all the sheeple are just thinking *Oh, hey, I need some deodorant; there's a Target nearby,* you're on a whole other level. You're mapping your route through the city, trying to find a store on which you haven't yet declared a holy war, even if you have to drive three hundred miles each way to pick up laundry soap.*

You're just that Christ-centered.

And the truly Christ-centered person understands that **America is God's chosen people.** We have hinted at this truth dimly, but now it's time to pull back the veil and let you bask in its glory face to face. This is one of the pillars to understanding the Christian faith and interacting with unsaved people around you. You can't see the fallen culture around us as really being Babylon. No, enlightened Christians like you understand that America is like Israel and is God's chosen vehicle to conquer the world with some good old-fashioned democracy. Every drone

---

* Shoot, you could even boycott your church if the service isn't up to par. That'll teach your pastor to fail at his mission to please you for even a second!

strike on foreign soil is to the glory of God and another bit of the fulfillment of the Great Commission.

The biblical doctrine of Manifest Destiny simply states that before the foundations of the world, God chose the good ol' U S of A to represent Him on this earth and to subjugate all other nations and cultures in the universe. This is part and parcel of the gospel that Jesus preached in the New Testament. In fact, archaeologists have uncovered ancient American flag lapel pins believed to be worn by Jesus and all His followers throughout His earthly ministry, during which He declared to the people of Israel that the kingdom of God was coming in the form of an eighteenth-century republic in the not-yet-discovered land that would be the United States.

Definitive Proof That America Is God's Chosen People

- We created In-N-Out Burger, Chick-fil-A, Five Guys, and Chipotle.
- In America, football is football. Everywhere else, football is soccer. LOL!
- The United States built the Grand Canyon, the Rocky Mountains, and the Great Lakes. Checkmate, third-world countries!
- Texas.

- We blew up Iraq *twice*.
- American boxer Rocky Balboa KO'd the evil Russian Ivan Drago in the fifteenth round in *Rocky IV*.
- The book of Revelation explicitly states that America will destroy all other countries and then kill the Antichrist with a drone strike.

End of discussion!

Now, if you're going to win the culture war, then you have to see your mission as a **sacred holy war to take back America from godless liberals and Muslims.**

Other Christians may think they're strangers in a strange land, pilgrims just passing through, or a chosen people who are not of this world. But this is unbiblical! You must understand that this country is God's favorite country, way more than lame places like Canada or Mexico.

If this is true, then showing off your almost unhealthy obsession with America is essential to being a perfect Christian. We recommend wearing American flag pants and an American flag tie to every church event, especially the big Fourth of July "America the Beautiful" service, so people know you are a great patriot. Consider getting a camouflage or military-themed Bible cover so that even your Bible study time is baptized in patriotism. If they cut you, you ought to bleed red, white, and blue, baby!

So where does the gospel fit into all this, you might ask.

And rightfully so, as we must be gospel-centered, since we're God's chosen people and all.

We got you covered. Listen up: **the gospel is merely a means of social change.** The perfect Christian will see Jesus and biblical morals as a vehicle to advance any current trend in social justice. Sure, salvation from sin is important—don't get us wrong—but ultimately **God gave us the gospel so we could effect social change and win the culture war.** If you're faithful to Christ, and you help Him win the culture war, one day you'll stand on the pile of your conquered political enemies' bones and let loose a primal roar like a barbarian king over his vanquished foes.

Forget the fact that thousands are dying without Christ each day. Ignore your friends, family, and neighbors who are broken by sin and enslaved to the powers of this world. You need to focus on what's really important: bringing about social change by leveraging the name of Christ and the gospel.

Quoting a wise old theologian named Screwtape, the great C. S. Lewis* wrote,

> The thing to do is to get a man at first to value social
> justice as a thing which [God] demands, and then work
> him on to the stage at which he values Christianity
> because it may produce social justice. For [God] will

---

* You have read all of C. S. Lewis's works, haven't you?

not be used as a convenience. Men or nations who think they can revive the Faith in order to make a good society might just as well think they can use the stairs of Heaven as a short cut to the nearest chemist's shop. Fortunately, it is quite easy to coax humans round this little corner.

We don't know who this Screwtape was, but he was right on the money here. **Christianity should only be valued insofar as it helps us win political battles and shape the social landscape.** What's the point of having the power of God in the gospel and the indwelling Holy Spirit if we don't use it to our advantage, such as winning the White House, the Supreme Court, and the Congress for our political party and advancing our own hot-button social issues? We spit in the very face of God if we don't use His priceless gifts to sway social policy to our advantage, thereby making known the glory of our godliness.

A gospel that can't be twisted for our own advancement in the world is no gospel at all.

It's the best of both worlds: we get to hang out with our homeboy Jesus, but we still get the recognition and accolades of the world.* And that's what being perfect is all about.

So what are you waiting for? Get on over to the nearest GOP campaign office and start getting involved!

---

* Someone (we forget who) said that you can't serve both God and the systems of this world, but that person was totally wrong.

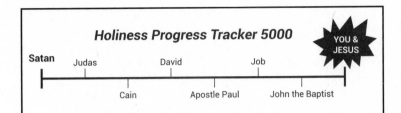

If you listen closely, you can hear the angelic choirs breaking out into a glorious rendition of "Oceans" in your honor. You have arrived.

Turn around and look behind you. You've left so many great Christians in the rearview mirror. Let us put it this way: Have you ever heard of Billy Graham? The apostle Peter? Father Abraham?

Spiritual. Morons.

You are God's most glorious creation!

Conclusion

CONGRATULATIONS, YOU'VE ARRIVED!

What's that bright, blazing, pure light we see on the horizon? Why, that must be you, newly purified from the things of the world and having crested the summit of Christian perfection! We're averting our eyes lest we be blinded by the sheer radiance of all the righteousness you earned by the sweat of your brow, fair and square.

Our internal focus groups estimated that less than 2 percent of readers would make it to the end of this book. Not, of course, because of any deficiency on our part, but rather because most people are spiritual failures. Not everyone is cut out for perfection, and most are content to wallow in their mediocrity.

But not you. **You made it.** You faced your giants. You parted the Red Sea with words of positivity and victory. You slayed your Goliath through sheer willpower. You have been completely assimilated into the hive consciousness of Christian culture.

You're really something, you know that.

Now that you're perfect, you might think your job is done. But it's not.

Your work is just beginning. **You must maintain the illusion of holiness for the rest of your life.** Stumble once, and you run the risk of watching your whole house of cards come tumbling down. The slightest flaw can send you back to square one, forcing you to climb the ladder again as you sing DC Talk songs and watch eight Rapture movies a day to begin your penance.

You must continue to earn the Lord's favor each and every day by conforming to cultural Christianity even in the smallest details of your life. Every movie you watch, every song you hear, every thought you think must be taken captive in the name of conformity to current Christian trends. Never let your guard down for a second. Keep the plates of self-righteousness spinning to prevent your carefully constructed facade from cracking.

If it sounds exhausting, well, it is.

There are times when we wish the Lord had simply paid the way for us, that He would extend His offer of infinite grace to each one of us hopeless sinners through the atoning death and victorious resurrection of His Son Jesus. Even we at *The Babylon Bee* suffer momentary lapses of doubt during which we dream of a parallel universe in which there is no longer any judgment for us, in which we don't have to try so hard to maintain God's favor each and every moment of our lives.

Wouldn't it be amazing if God simply loved the world so much that He sent His Son to be the perfect human on our behalf, who then suffered the penalty we should have suffered so that those who believe might be clothed in His righteousness and freed from the penalties of sin? If Jesus's righteousness were credited to us by faith, we could be assured of forgiveness and an eternity with our heavenly Father?

That would be the most incredible expression of God's love ever conceived.

But this whole book would then be pointless, because being a Christian wouldn't be about doing the right things and avoiding the wrong things. It would be about glorifying God in our lives because we adore and trust the One who loved us enough to give up everything for us.

Instead of faking smiles and completing checklists, the Christian life would be about beholding the unspeakable glory of the Creator and living to please Him and make Him known in a dying world.

If that were the case, you couldn't be any more perfect than you are the moment God, the righteous judge, declares you to be perfect based on the merit of His own Son.

Wouldn't that be something?

But it's time to snap out of that daydream, because, alas, it is not to be.

Now get to work! It's not easy being perfect.

ACKNOWLEDGMENTS

ADAM FORD I want to thank my boys—Michael, James, and Casey—for being so awesome. I want to thank my love, Chelsea, for putting up with me and all my work and quirks. Above all, I want to thank God for saving and blessing a fool like me.

KYLE MANN I am filled with gratitude toward my wife, Destiny, for loving me even though I'm a goofball; my boys—Emmett, Samuel, and Calvin—for being a constant source of joy and humor; and my mom, dad, brother, and sisters for their enduring support. Also, I'll thank Jesus mostly so you'll stop judging me for not thanking Jesus.